entertaining
in the raw

entertaining
in the raw

matthew kenney
photography by miha matei

GIBBS SMITH
TO ENRICH AND INSPIRE HUMANKIND
Salt Lake City | Charleston | Santa Fe | Santa Barbara

First Edition

5 4 3 2 1   13 12 11 10 09

Published by
Gibbs Smith
P.O. Box 667
Layton, Utah 84041

Orders: 1.800.835.4993
www.gibbs-smith.com

Designed by Debra McQuiston
Printed and bound in China
Gibbs Smith books are printed on either recycled, 100% post-
consumer waste, or FSC-certified papers.

Library of Congress Cataloging-in-Publication Data
Kenney, Matthew.
Entertaining in the raw / Matthew Kenney ;
photographs by Miha Matei. — 1st ed.
p. cm.
Includes index.
ISBN-13: 978-1-4236-0208-8
ISBN-10: 1-4236-0208-0
1. Cookery (Natural foods) 2. Raw foods. 3. Entertaining.
4. Cookery, International. I. Title.
TX741.K46 2009
641.5'636—dc22
2008030784

to my parents, **shirley and robert kenney**

contents

Introduction   11

Blossom   19

Contemporary   53

Inspiration   85

Spice   111

Radiance   143

Revolution   175

Meaningful   209

Index   234

I believe that if one
always looked at the skies,
one would end up with wings.

—Gustave Flaubert

acknowledgments

My life has been blessed with inspiration and support from many talented people. I would like to thank:

Liz Figueroa, for her love.

Miha Matei, the best photographer I have ever met.

Maryellen and Paul Schoeman, and Patrick Kenney, who I am proud to have as family.

Lenny Lagana, for friendship and words of wisdom.

Kristen Reyes and Andrew Tupper, for their hard work and creativity.

Anna Elisa de Castro, for her styling brilliance.

Michelle Witte and Jennifer Grillone, my editors, for their patience and skilled guidance.

Jennifer King, Christopher Robbins and the entire team at Gibbs Smith, Publisher, for being true partners.

Gibbs Smith, an incredible visionary, whose company I am fortunate to work with.

Peter Schatzberg, a warrior, both as a friend and a business partner.

Leo Monroy, Michael Schatzberg and the team at Freefoods, for their dedication to excellence.

Chase's Daily, a miracle in Maine.

Debra McQuiston, for her impeccable design skills.

the goal of life is living in agreement with nature.

—Zeno (335–264 BC)

introduction

Entertain—The first time I stepped into a raw food kitchen, I knew that I had discovered something magical. My senses had been on high alert as I remained deeply suspicious about uncooked food, and many years in professional kitchens had created a foundation of principles contrary to what I was about to experience. Yet I nearly became an instant convert, ready to forgo not only fire and heat but also the majority of ingredients that were the building blocks of my cuisine.

To this day, I still remain captivated by steaming pots of risotto, the hearty aromas of a wood-fired oven, and the intense flavor brought on by a long-simmering reduction. Yet nothing has ever captured my attention in a kitchen like the crisp smell of fresh ginger mingling with coriander and lime juice, as I entered that day. And nothing has held it like the explosive clean flavor of well-prepared raw organic foods.

My first year of preparing raw was somewhat challenging. Just as I was entering a phase of my career where the skills I had learned and experiences I had accumulated should have provided me with the tools I needed to cook at a higher, more mature level, I chose to discard everything and begin anew. Fortunately, it was a natural decision, taken not only for professional and creative reasons but also in light of my own personal preferences, which had begun to lean more and more toward a plant-based lifestyle. The choice led me to the most rewarding and creative experience of my life.

In the beginning, just as with traditional European-based cuisine, it was necessary to learn the basics. Instead of stocks and bases, searing and braising, I needed to experiment with Brazil nut milk and vegetable juice–based sauces and to focus on marinating and dehydrating as ways to intensify flavor. In the beginning, there were a few triumphs and many failures; but as I experimented more, dishes began to emerge that would open up a raw food world of unlimited potential. At Pure Food and Wine, the first raw food restaurant I built, early recipes such as Heirloom Tomato Lasagna would become popular signatures, providing colorful and tasty dishes that were not incredibly difficult to prepare. And over the first year there, other experiments that I had begun, such as White Corn Tamale with Raw Cacao Mole, were flushed out by talented cooks. The menu evolved to include some of these earlier, more straightforward dishes as well as a handful of newer, more complex ones.

Over the next two years, I would begin to delineate two styles of raw food preparation: practical dishes that are faster to prepare at home or for a quick meal, and more elaborate dishes that require a bit more patience and effort. Those more elaborate dishes are in large part what make raw food so remarkable. The health benefits and flavors of everyday raw food are incredible on many levels. As a chef, I am most inspired by the tastes, textures, and presentation of the more advanced recipes.

There is no denying that some of the best raw food dishes are downright challenging to prepare. Several steps may be involved, often beginning with "sprouting" nuts, seeds, or grains, and ending with as much as forty-eight hours of dehydration. Others may provide a bit more instant gratification. This book is written in honor of the more elaborate, but very worthwhile, recipes that challenge the cook and please the guest. The attention, persistence, and care that go into the recipes in this book deserve to be celebrated and enjoyed by those who are fortunate enough to eat them.

whether it is an extravagant wedding dinner on an exotic beach or dinner for two by candlelight, the impact and pleasures of raw food are, by and large, incomparable to other challengers.

Share—In my earlier days with raw food, I often found myself shying away from preparing it for family and friends, instead finding a middle ground with perhaps vegetarian or vegan dishes. Over time, as my food evolved, I became more confident about people's reaction to this incredible cuisine, and now I prepare it whenever I have the opportunity. In fact, I firmly believe that it is often the best choice of food to entertain with. Whether it is an extravagant wedding dinner on an exotic beach or dinner for two by candlelight, the impact and pleasures of raw food are, by and large, incomparable to other challengers.

No other culinary style offers the same vibrant, deep flavor without guilt or other effects that celebratory foods often have, such as a heavy feeling or fatigue. Raw food is the most colorful on the planet—it literally jumps off the plate! Raw is very modern, forgoing heavy sauces, dairy products, and breads, allowing each bite to pack maximum flavor. In every one of my raw dining experiences, I have found that the food ends up not only being enjoyed but also being used as a conversational piece, where guests marvel at their surprise to learn the food before them is composed of fruits, vegetables, nuts, and seeds, none of which have been cooked, canned, or processed in any way.

Some of the ideas are pretty "out there"—think Willy Wonka's chocolate or Andy Warhol's art factory, where unbounded creativity exists in an effort to pursue meaning and, in this case, the essence of raw food. My philosophy is guided by one stipulation: all of the culinary efforts shall be devoted to preparing the most advanced, flavorful, and realistic raw food anywhere. As long as my work considers those fundamental issues, I allow pretty much free reign to spontaneously experiment and create. The results should entertain not only the guests but also the cook.

Plan—This book represents that philosophy and the results of freethinking that has always kept a sharp eye out for flavor, presentation, and originality. At the end of the day, it's all a good meal—and a good meal should never be eaten alone.

There is always much more to entertaining than the food. With raw food, it's even truer, and many of the "traditional" rules change. That should never be seen as a barrier but, rather, as an opportunity. Raw food is vegetarian and, when handled by responsible chefs, is largely produced from organic ingredients in a sustainable environment. The location and setting of a raw food meal need not be elaborate, but it should respect nature, and any additions to the setting are most appropriate when they also show the same respect. Natural materials, fresh wildflowers or bamboo, clean design, and plate settings are all more appropriate than leather or over-designed cutlery and china. The best rule of thumb is to always consider nature—if something is a step removed from nature, it's probably suitable. If you don't know how it is made, then it's probably not.

Ingredients are always the most important part of a great meal. This holds even truer with raw food, where nothing will be masked by flour, sugar, butter, or heavy cooking. It is always worth the effort to search for the freshest organic ingredients—local if at all possible. Many raw food recipes require soaking, sprouting, marinating, and dehydrating. For that reason, it is best to sit down with the recipes you intend to prepare and make two lists: one for shopping and another for preparation. The great thing about raw food is its versatility as to when it needs to be served. Whereas some cooked food often becomes dry or inedible if not eaten when it is finished cooking, the recipes in this book that won't hold up for a very long time are designed to be prepared ahead but assembled when ready to eat. Many of the most complicated dishes can actually be plated and garnished in no time, as long as the preparation (what chefs call *mis en place*) is in good order.

Raw food provides many opportunities for service that other foods don't. It does not need to be hot, although a few dishes are recommended to be served slightly warm from the dehydrator, which can sometimes maximize flavor and texture. For this reason, it is an ideal choice for an outdoor meal or a meal in a space with no traditional kitchen. The only requirement in most cases would be to have nearby access to electricity in case something needs to be warmed, blended, or finished at the last minute.

It is always a good idea to consider the balance of dishes that are served. My chapters provide some guidance in this area and highlight ways that food can be combined to make a statement beyond just taste. All of the recipes in this book are inspired by a season, emotion, or other value that relates to experimental cuisine. I believe that food for entertaining is more interesting if it relates to something larger, just as the best art and literature always offer a message beyond their respective beauty or story. A menu concept can be as straightforward as "summer" and as elaborate as something inspired by contemporary art. These concepts also provide more for guests to indulge in and will surprise the cook in how they also give a deeper appreciation for the food itself. Whereas French cuisine, for example, has centuries of history behind it, upscale raw food is relatively new, and these creative attachments help build its core personality.

Enjoy—As a home or professional cook, perhaps the greatest reward with this food is that you will have a better opportunity to be with your guests, because the food does not have to be warmed, reduced, heated, and taken out of the oven. Assuming the mis en place is taken care of, assembly is still required, but it will be much faster than usual to finalize the plates. Most of these recipes are not portioned in a traditional way, meaning that they provide the flexibility to be served on smaller plates or larger platters or, in most cases, at a large decorated table. They hold up well and many don't need to be eaten right away. Having no pots and pans to wash is perhaps the final surprise.

On my own journey with raw food, I found challenge, excitement, flavor, health, and a new sense of creative direction. If this book offers you the same rewards, I think you'll be well fed—and happy.

Guidance—Every book has a story—where its idea originated, what the message is, and how it should be used on a day-to-day basis. In writing this one, although the book has developed a personality of its own over time, my goal has always been to bring to life the many unique possibilities that raw food beholds. I am so personally impressed by raw food, and inspired on a regular basis, that I instinctively knew the kind of book I wanted to write from the beginning. Putting the words and recipes together was a far more complicated process, but it still happened naturally. The result is a very personal expression of how raw food fits into our daily lives, not only from a culinary but also an emotional perspective. In order to use Entertaining in the Raw most effectively, it would be beneficial to adapt your own personal approach to the information it offers. Allow my recipes and suggestions to serve as a guideline, always remembering that you are the chef in your kitchen. I offer a few suggestions as to how you may enjoy your experience even more.

Recipes are like roadmaps: They may offer the fastest way to arrive at a result, but your trip must take into account personal tastes, your schedule and sometimes even the weather. Although I may like something spicy, you may prefer it a bit sweet, or a dish that I've recommend you serve in a composed manner might be more appealing to you with its components kept separate. Time is something that we all value and never seem to have enough of. Therefore, it is always necessary with detailed recipes such as these, to read a recipe in its entirety, think about your approach and make decisions about what can be done ahead, of if there is a component you'd like to leave out. My comment about the weather is a very real one: humidity or dryness affects the texture of many raw food recipes and can dramatically alter dehydrating times, crispness, and even taste of some dishes. An ingredient in one part of the world may look the same but taste totally different than one from afar. Be open-minded and try to take the best route for you.

Think of this book as you might about fashion, creating your own combinations to suit personal tastes and preferences. There are really several recipes within each dish—dozens of sauces, garnishes, fillings, bases, and other elements. Each of these can be used as part of a meal, as an addition to a salad or dessert, or in any number of ways. My best suggestion is to read this book in its entirety, cover to cover, and get familiar with it, just like you might your own wardrobe. Think of it and all of its elements as part of your culinary arsenal and make use of it accordingly. Most of dishes in this book are structured as they would be in a restaurant environment or at an important event or celebration. Still, the basic elements and techniques of the book are all applicable on a regular basis, and can be used in the same way that much simpler recipes might be. Ideally, as a reader of the book, you will feel that your possibilities for raw food preparation have been expanded.

Every meal is a unique experience and, therefore, a recipe is simply a tool to help enhance that experience. While I have suggested how to present my recipes with photographs and assembly instructions, you may prefer to serve everything family style. Tacos, for example, would be great with the components in separate bowls and the naked shells available for everyone to choose from. Let guests fill them, make them part of that experience, and it usually works out well. I may use a garnish that you don't have access to—it's only a garnish, but changing a green, or removing spice here and there, will not seriously compromise a dish. You will often have leftover sauces or fillings. Some recipes are easier to produce in larger quantities and don't work well in very small batches due to equipment limitations or other reasons. That said, I've never seen an extra cup or two of chocolate sauce, marshmallow cream, or raw ice cream go to waste. In fact, it may just be good for breakfast.

Just remember, it's about the experience, not only with what's on the plate, but how you arrived at the plate. If you've enjoyed it to that stage, you'll have a great meal.

if nothing ever changed, there'd be no butterflies.

—Tom Robbins, *Still Life with Woodpecker*

blossom

Every spring, I encounter a moment where I am transported back to my childhood during an unseasonably warm afternoon on the coast of Maine. It is really a sensation of earthy aroma: the warming sun combined with thawing soil, as if the light is melting away winter. Like no other place, Maine embraces each season with abandon and teaches its inhabitants not to hold on for too long, but to savor it while it lasts. When I first began my journey as a chef, I lacked many of the tools that some of my colleagues had: a tradition of a family with a deeply rooted culinary background, lifelong access to specialty markets and restaurants, growing up as a gourmand. In fact, Searsport, Maine, is far better known for its quaint coastal charm than for any of its culinary aptitude. Still, I was fortunate to have a childhood that taught me more about seasonality than all of my future years of cooking combined.

In the summer, I could walk across the street from my home to the edge of the field in front of Penobscot Bay and pick tiny, sweet wild strawberries, blackberries, and raspberries directly from their vines. My grandfather's cherry tree provided sweet fruit for eating, with pits to launch at my cousins. My dad would navigate our way across a fast-flowing river onto his "mountain," where we would forage fiddlehead ferns in the wild. We always had a garden, and the memories are secure in my mind . . . taste of earth, aroma of sun, crisp, watery, and colorful—husking corn, shelling peas, even the rattling cover of my mom's cookware as the water heated to cook the summer vegetables.

As time has passed, my appreciation for seasonal produce has only expanded. As a chef, I learned to become excited about autumn mushrooms, the first early asparagus and green garlic, even the cool of winter when citrus fruits and root vegetables provide a new culinary challenge . . . beets and orange zest, with a little pistachio oil and sea salt . . . it all makes sense and is the way we should be eating.

With raw food, the emphasis on seasonality is even more important. There is no smoky grill to mask the essence of the ingredients, no deep-frying that really strips rather than adds flavor. This is naked cuisine—presented in its purest form, creatively combined, but with its character always retained. A cook has nothing greater to celebrate than the seasons.

In time, a seasoned chef will expend the same effort—perhaps more—in sourcing ingredients as in preparing them. If I were to make a Moroccan tagine for dinner on a fall evening in New York, it could mean biking to the Greenmarket for autumn squash and pumpkin, visiting Sahadi's (my favorite Middle Eastern market) for pomegranates and almonds, crossing the bridge to Kalustyan's for spices, and on it goes. No amount of diligence will ever be too much.

As with food, entertaining is always most appropriate when it follows the arc of the seasons. Cherry and apple blossoms on their branches, baskets of brown pears, sugar pumpkins, crab apples, and fresh wildflowers are only a fraction of what is available for us when setting a table or creating a room that evokes seasonality. The same influences that guide our menu choices provide elegant nuances to luscious cocktails and cool beverages. I am so enamored with seasonality, embracing each one with such passion, that the onset of longer days and brighter sun, the cool crisp breeze of an approaching winter, or the quiet lazy days of summer are each worthy of throwing a long lunch, a dinner, or a cocktail party. We may as well enjoy them before they pass. And just as you become enamored with those beautiful heirloom tomatoes, they will disappear.

sweet pea flan with macadamia foam, lime powder, and black sesame tuile

When my team and I first plated it, I experienced the rush that accompanies an intense creative effort that ends in success. The colors are remarkable, and it is every bit as silky and smooth as a flan should be. It is one of my most highly recommended dishes for a dinner party that includes many guests who are new to raw.

FLAN
3 cups cashews, soaked 1–2 hours
$1/2$ cup coconut meat
$1/4$ cup prepared Irish moss
$1/4$ cup juice of sugar snap peas
$1/2$ teaspoon salt
8 large fresh mint leaves

FOAM
1 cup macadamia nuts, soaked 1–2 hours
3 cups water
Salt
Soy lecithin

LIME POWDER
1 pint lime zest

TUILE
$1/4$ cup ground black sesame seeds
$1/2$ cup flax meal
$1/2$ cup chopped yellow squash
1 tablespoon lemon juice
1 cup water
1 tablespoon raw agave
$1/2$ teaspoon salt
$1/4$ teaspoon coriander seeds
$1/2$ teaspoon ground cumin

FLAN Blend all ingredients in a Vita-Mix until very smooth. Pour into lightly oiled flan or custard ramekins and place in the refrigerator for at least 1 hour, until firm.

FOAM Blend all ingredients in Vita-Mix until smooth; strain through a chinois and reserve.

LIME POWDER Spread zest on Teflex sheets and cover with a dehydrator screen. Dehydrate overnight until completely dry. Place in Vita-Mix and blend into a powder.

TUILE Place ground sesame seeds in a large bowl; set aside. Blend remaining ingredients in Vita-Mix until smooth.

Combine mixture with the sesame seeds. Spread over Teflex sheets in a very thin layer. Dehydrate 6–8 hours until dry but still very pliable. Cut into long thin triangles. Arrange each over cylinder shapes, such as a rolling pin, on dehydrator trays; dehydrate until crisp.

ASSEMBLY Use a small offset spatula to loosen sides of flan and turn out onto a serving dish. Place a tuile near the flan. Blend macadamia foam, 2–3 cups at a time, in Vita-Mix. Spoon foam from top of mixture and drizzle close to flan, hugging the edges, for garnish. Sprinkle with lime powder. SERVES 4–6

yellow corn chowder

This is not exactly the version that I would often enjoy during July and August while growing up in Maine, but it does capture the creamy sweet richness of traditional summer corn chowder. When I first served this, it was everyone's favorite dish that evening—and it is easy enough to make ahead and warm a bit in the dehydrator or to serve chilled on a sultry day.

CHOWDER
4 cups yellow corn
$^3/_4$ cup young coconut meat
$2^1/_2$ cups cashew milk (made from 3 cups water plus 2 cups cashews, soaked)
1 tablespoon plus 1 teaspoon salt
Black pepper

$2^1/_4$ teaspoons ancho chili powder
3 tablespoons olive oil
$^1/_4$ cup raw agave
$^1/_2$ cup coconut water

GARNISH
$^1/_2$ cup fresh corn kernels
1 tablespoon finely chopped fresh tarragon

CHOWDER Blend all ingredients in a Vita-Mix until smooth.

ASSEMBLY Divide chowder into four small bowls. Add the whole corn into the soup by hand. Garnish with fresh tarragon. **SERVES 4**

cream of matsutake soup, pignoli dumplings, pears, and tarragon

The matsutake is highly valued by the Japanese—and for good reason. It is said to be an aphrodisiac and has a wonderful nutty, spicy flavor. Matsutake, also known as the pine mushroom, grow under pine trees that are between twenty and sixty years old, and never in the same place twice. These mushrooms are said to be high in vitamins and low in calories, and are thought to prevent aging. Most of all, I love their taste. This recipe is my favorite of all the raw soups I have had—it is extremely decadent, elegant, and refined, a wonderfully earthy and filling dish.

FILLING
1 cup pine nuts, soaked 1–2 hours
1 tablespoon lemon juice
$^1/_2$ teaspoon salt
1 teaspoon nutritional yeast
2 tablespoons scallions

WRAPPERS
2 cups coconut meat
$^1/_4$ cup spinach juice
$^1/_4$ teaspoon sea salt
1 bunch chives

SOUP
About 20 matsutake mushrooms, cut from stem, divided
Salt
Olive oil
2 cups pine nuts, soaked 1–2 hours
6 cups water
$^1/_4$ cup white miso
1 tablespoon chopped fresh tarragon
2 tablespoons soy lecithin
Black pepper

GARNISH
1 pear, cut into matchsticks
Olive oil
Black pepper
Fresh tarragon leaves

FILLING Process all ingredients in a food processor until smooth.

WRAPPERS Blend all ingredients except chives in a Vita-Mix until smooth. Spread thin on Teflex sheets. Dehydrate 4–5 hours until dry but still very flexible. Trim edges and cut into 9 squares per sheet. Place small amount of filling in center of wrapper; pull up edges around cheese and form a beggar's purse. Tie to secure with a chive.

SOUP Toss mushrooms with salt and enough olive oil to lightly coat them. Blend pine nuts, water, salt, miso, tarragon, and soy lecithin until smooth. Strain through a chinois. Spread on Teflex sheets; dehydrate 1–2 hours. Blend $^3/_4$ of the mushrooms with the puréed ingredients and reserve the remainder for garnish. Season with salt and black pepper to taste.

ASSEMBLY Pour the soup in deep bowls. Float two dumplings in the center, garnishing around it with pear matchsticks. Drizzle with a touch of olive oil, top with freshly cracked black pepper, and garnish with tarragon leaves and remaining mushrooms. SERVES 4

ragout of spring vegetables, chanterelle essence, and pignoli "parmesan" crisp

Delicate is not a word I associated with raw food early on. Many of the original dishes I tasted or prepared were quite hearty, bolstered by the presence of nuts and crunchy textures. A typical sauce would be a pesto, chutney, or vegetable purée. As time went on, I started to experiment with broths and lightening the food. For one spring dinner, I wanted to capture not only that season's essence in the use of ingredients we chose but also its texture and weight overall. As a result, I discovered that lightly "poaching" in a dehydrator created the effect I had been missing, and I've made ample use of it ever since. This style of dish is great for a dinner party, as it is very easy to prepare in advance and serve when needed.

RAGOUT BROTH
4 cups cucumber juice
4 cups celery juice
Salt
1 tablespoon cracked black peppercorns
$1/4$ cup chopped shallots
$1/4$ cup chopped fresh thyme
$1/4$ cup chopped fresh rosemary
$1/2$ bunch pencil asparagus, sliced on a bias into
   $11/2$-inch lengths
3 cups sliced almond mushroom caps (reserve stems for sauce)
1 cup halved cherry tomatoes
1 fennel bulb, cored and sliced

RAGOUT SAUCE
1 cup almonds, soaked 2 hours
3 cups water

Salt
1 tablespoon soy lecithin
Almond mushroom stems
Olive oil

ESSENCE
2 cups chanterelle mushrooms

CRISPS
1 quart pine nuts, soaked 1–2 hours
$1/2$ cup lemon juice
$1/4$ cup nutritional yeast
2 teaspoons salt
2 cups water
2 tablespoons chopped fresh thyme
$1/2$ cup chopped scallions

GARNISH
$1/4$ cup fresh chervil leaves

RAGOUT BROTH Mix the first seven ingredients in a bowl. Place asparagus, mushroom caps, tomatoes, and fennel separately in half sheet pans or shallow cooking pans; pour broth over vegetables. Place in bottom of dehydrators at 115 degrees F and let "poach" 2–3 hours.

RAGOUT SAUCE Blend almonds, water, salt, and soy lecithin; strain through a fine chinois. Toss mushroom stems in olive oil and salt; place on dehydrator Teflex sheets and dehydrate 1 hour. Add marinated mushrooms to almond mixture and blend in a Vita-Mix until smooth.

ESSENCE Place mushrooms on dehydrator screens and dehydrate until crisp. Blend in Vita-Mix until fine powder forms.

CRISPS Process first five ingredients in a food processor until smooth. Add thyme and scallions and pulse until well combined. Spread mixture onto Teflex sheets; dehydrate overnight until crisp. Break into large shards for garnish.

ASSEMBLY Divide the vegetables among shallow bowls and pour $1/2$ cup sauce over each. Sprinkle generously with mushroom essence, garnish with crisps and chervil. SERVES 4

basil raviolini with summer tomato sauce

I used to love garlic so much that I would come home from working a sixteen-hour day and prepare risotto at midnight, carefully stirring, adding stock (and usually wild mushrooms, which I still love today), and finishing with several cloves of roasted garlic or, even better, elephant garlic. I couldn't get enough. And somewhere along the palate path, I developed an aversion to it. There seem to be a few schools of thought on garlic—some feel that it is therapeutic and others that it is toxic. I am now of the latter, although I would never dispute the fact that it tastes great. While mature garlic takes away some of the cleaner flavors that I so admire in raw food, young garlic and garlic flowers are more subtle—enough so that I was very happy to serve this dish at one of my dinners.

RAVIOLINI WRAPPERS
(see page 30)

RAVIOLINI PURÉE
1 cup almond meal (blend 3 cups sprouted almonds
  with 2 cups water and squeeze all liquid out of the
  purée—dehydrate the solids on a Teflex sheet for 12
  hours, remove from sheet onto screen and dehydrate
  another 24 hours; let cool. Stored tightly, this will keep
  for a couple of weeks in a cool place.)
$1/2$ cup pine nuts, soaked 1–2 hours
$1/2$ cup cashews, soaked 1–2 hours
2 tablespoons lemon juice
$2^1/2$ teaspoons salt

2 teaspoons nutritional yeast
$1/4$ cup olive oil
$1/4$ cup garlic scapes or young green garlic
$1/2$ cup finely chopped fresh basil

SAUCE
$1/4$ cup olive oil
3 cups chopped heirloom or red beefsteak tomatoes
Pinch red chili flakes
Salt and pepper to taste
$1/4$ cup julienned fresh oregano

GARNISH
Fresh oregano leaves

RAVIOLINI PURÉE Blend all ingredients except basil in a food processor until very smooth. Stir in basil by hand.

SAUCE Toss olive oil and tomatoes together in a bowl. Place bowl in a dehydrator for 1–2 hours. Blend dehydrated tomatoes and chili flakes in a Vita-Mix until very smooth, season with salt and pepper, and stir in oregano.

ASSEMBLY Place 1 tablespoon of purée on $1/2$ the wrappers and spread it to $1/4$ inch from the sides. Brush the corners

with a touch of water and press another wrapper on top, tightly holding it together.

To serve, cover the bottom of a plate with tomato sauce and set 4 raviolini on each plate. Garnish with fresh oregano leaves. **SERVES 4**

basil black pepper wrappers, macadamia "cheese," cherry tomatoes, and avocado

The discovery of using young coconut as a wrapper and all-purpose replacement for pasta and rice paper was a miracle for us at my former restaurant the Plant. We have since evolved to using it in many forms, colors, and flavors, with this dish being one of my favorites. Often the best dishes are those that are somehow familiar to us, and I don't know anyone who doesn't like tomato and basil together. These are also great for entertaining because the components can be made in advance and assembled by the guests or just before serving. They're addictively delicious.

WRAPPERS
4 cups coconut meat
$1/4$ cup spinach juice
1 cup fresh basil leaves
$1/4$ teaspoon salt
$1/2$ teaspoon coarsely ground black pepper

"CHEESE"
2 cups macadamia nuts, soaked 1–2 hours
2 tablespoons lemon juice
1 tablespoon nutritional yeast

$1/2$ medium-size shallot
$3/4$ teaspoon salt

DRIED CHERRY TOMATOES
1 cup halved ripe cherry tomatoes
Olive oil
Pinch salt

GARNISH
Basil leaves
1 avocado, halved, pitted, and thinly sliced

WRAPPERS Blend all ingredients except black pepper until very smooth. Spread very thin on Teflex sheets, sprinkle with the black pepper, and dehydrate 3–4 hours. Remove from Teflex and trim edges. Cut in 9 squares and reserve. They hold best when placed between wax paper and kept cool.

"CHEESE" Process all ingredients in a food processor until well combined. Crumble mixture onto dehydrator screens and dehydrate 4–6 hours. Store in refrigerator.

DRIED CHERRY TOMATOES Toss the cherry tomatoes with olive oil and salt, and spread on dehydrator screens. Dehydrate 3–4 hours. Remove and set aside at room temperature.

ASSEMBLY Place the wrappers flat on a work surface. Put 1 teaspoon "cheese" in the center of each wrapper and top with avocado, cherry tomatoes, and a fresh basil leaf. Lightly wet two of the opposite corners with a touch of water and roll them from one side, with the corner just reaching over the filling. Roll the other corner over that, forming a boat shape. Press tightly so they remain together.
SERVES 4–6

squash blossoms with pistachio purée, green zebra fondue, pine nuts, and purple basil

For a raw chef, summer means outdoor farmers markets, and also food with tremendous vibrancy and color that can be easier to prepare than more elaborate winter dishes. Everyone generally thinks of squash blossoms as a dish that is stuffed (sometimes with cheese, crab, or pork), battered, and fried. Admittedly, they can be delicious in their traditional form, but they are also just as tasty raw and are a great carrier for other summer flavors—this dish combines so many of my favorite ingredients that I can easily make a meal from it. The green zebra fondue was an experiment that rewarded me with a new way to make sauces, and is one that I'll use over and over again.

SQUASH BLOSSOMS
24 stemmed and cleaned squash blossoms (carefully clean and wash blossoms, leaving less than 1 inch of stem)

PURÉE
3 cups pistachios, soaked 1–2 hours
1/4 cup lemon juice
1/2 cup water
1/2 cup olive oil
2 1/2 teaspoons salt

2 teaspoons nutritional yeast
2 tablespoons raw agave

FONDUE
1/4 cup olive oil
3 cups chopped green zebra tomatoes
Salt and pepper to taste
1/4 cup julienned basil

GARNISH
1 1/4 cups roughly chopped pine nuts
Purple basil leaves

PURÉE Process ingredients in a food processor 3–5 minutes until smooth.

FONDUE Toss olive oil and tomatoes together in a bowl. Place bowl in a dehydrator for 1–2 hours. Blend all ingredients in a Vita-Mix until very smooth, season with salt and pepper, and stir in basil.

ASSEMBLY Stuff the squash blossoms with purée until plump. Divide the fondue and place on the bottom of each plate. Top each with 6 squash blossoms. Garnish with chopped pine nuts and purple basil. **SERVES 4**

ginger cantaloupe "gelato" and watermelon granité with muscat honeydew purée

Back in the day when I used to be a frequent restaurant patron, I would go to great lengths to dine at New York's best restaurants. The original Bouley in Tribeca was a phenomenal place, with food and décor that were always magical. David Bouley, the chef and owner, offered each guest a special dish after main courses, just before dessert. It was light melon soup with some of the lightest sorbets I have ever had. The combination of two soft cool textures together is something I never forgot—this dish is inspired by that.

"GELATO"
1/2 cup cashews, soaked 1–2 hours
1 cup macadamia nuts, soaked 1–2 hours
1/4 cup coconut meat
3/4 cup raw agave
2 1/2 cups cantaloupe juice
1/4 cup ginger juice
2 teaspoons vanilla extract
Pinch sea salt
1/4 cup coconut oil

GRANITÉ
1 medium-size ripe watermelon
1/4 cup raw agave

PURÉE
1/2 cup semisweet white wine, preferably Riesling
1 honeydew melon, seeded and blended
1/4 cup raw agave
1 vanilla bean, scraped
1/4 teaspoon salt

GARNISH
Fresh mint leaves, lavender sprigs, or edible flowers

"GELATO" Blend all ingredients in a Vita-Mix until smooth. Pour into an ice cream maker and freeze according to manufacturer's directions.

GRANITÉ Mash watermelon through a medium chinois. Add agave and freeze in a shallow pan. Allow the top to begin to freeze, about 2 hours, then lightly mash with a fork. Continue this every couple of hours until the mixture is frozen and flaky.

PURÉE Blend all ingredients in Vita-Mix until very smooth.

ASSEMBLY Place two scoops of "gelato" and one scoop of granité in each of four bowls. Pour enough honeydew purée into each bowl to reach halfway up the sides of the "gelato." Float a few mint leaves or flowers in the purée for garnish. **SERVES 4–6**

frozen chocolate pudding with cinnamon-glazed plums, chocolate basil wafers, and vanilla bean–plum syrup

I dare anyone not to like chocolate and plums. Is that even possible? It seems that everyone loves chocolate these days. I like to combine it with seasonal fruits, particularly stone fruits, which provide a good balance with their tartness and also a slightly nontraditional pairing.

PUDDING
2 cups cashews, soaked 1–2 hours
2 cups coconut meat
1 cup water
1^1/$_4$ cups raw agave
1 cup coconut oil
1 teaspoon vanilla extract
^{1}/$_2$ teaspoon sea salt
1^1/$_4$ cups cacao powder
2 tablespoons raw carob powder

PLUMS
1 cup raw agave
3 tablespoons ginger juice
2 teaspoons ground cinnamon
^{1}/$_2$ teaspoon ground star anise
Pinch salt
8 plums, various sizes and colors if possible, halved, pitted, and cut into eighths

WAFERS
2^1/$_2$ cups cashew flour
1^3/$_4$ cups oat flour
1^1/$_2$ teaspoons sea salt
^{1}/$_4$ cup water
1 cup maple syrup
1 cup cocoa powder
^{1}/$_2$ cup packed fresh basil leaves
1 tablespoon vanilla extract

SYRUP
1 cup raw agave
1^1/$_2$ cups pitted and chopped sugar plums
^{1}/$_4$ teaspoon salt
1 vanilla bean, scraped
2 tablespoons vanilla extract

GARNISH
Fresh mint sprigs

PUDDING Blend all ingredients in a Vita-Mix until completely smooth. Pour into a half sheet or low-sided baking dish and chill in freezer until firm.

PLUMS Blend all ingredients except plums in Vita-Mix until smooth. Toss with plums in a shallow baking dish and set aside at room temperature.

WAFERS Mix flours and sea salt in a medium-size bowl. Blend the remaining ingredients in Vita-Mix until smooth. Add to flour mixture and mix well with hands. Spread very thin long rectangles on Teflex sheets and dehydrate 6 hours. Turn onto screens and dehydrate until crisp, another 8–12 hours.

SYRUP Blend until smooth in Vita-Mix. Strain through a fine chinois.

ASSEMBLY Place a 3-inch ring mold in the center of a plate and scoop enough chocolate pudding into it until 2 inches high. Press top with a spoon to pack it and smooth the top. Remove ring carefully. Top with a pile of plums (they should be naturally piled on top; if some are falling, that is fine). Spoon generous amounts of the plum syrup around the plate and garnish with mint sprigs and wafers. **SERVES 4–6**

marinated tomato salad, pine nut "parmesan," basil oil, micro greens, and black pepper

Farmers markets embody summer, and New York now has a very passionate audience that patronizes them. The Union Square Greenmarket may be the most well known, but when I was living in Brooklyn, I began to visit the one in Park Slope, on the edge of Prospect Park. It is not the largest in the city, but it is quite substantial and the products are amazing. It was there that I found some of the most beautiful tomatoes of my life, bursting with color, with flavor so intense that you could almost taste the sun inside each bite. I also purchased several varieties of basil for the best tomato salad I've ever had.

TOMATOES
1/4 cup olive oil
2 tablespoons raw agave
Salt
Black pepper
1 1/2 pounds halved red, yellow, and green cherry tomatoes

"PARMESAN"
2 cups pine nuts
1/2 cup water

1 teaspoon olive oil
1 tablespoon sea salt
2 tablespoons lemon juice
2 tablespoons nutritional yeast

OIL
1 bunch fresh basil leaves
1 cup pure olive oil

GARNISH
Fresh basil sprigs
Salt and pepper

TOMATOES Mix all ingredients together.

"PARMESAN" Process all ingredients in a food processor until well combined. Spread in 1/8-inch-thick slices on Teflex sheets in a dehydrator and heat until it becomes firm, about 12 hours. Turn over Parmesan sheets onto dehydrator screens and continue dehydrating for 24 hours. Remove, let cool, and break into 2- or 3-inch shards. Keep covered.

OIL Place basil leaves in a blender with the olive oil. Purée until smooth. Place in a bowl or low-sided pan and put into dehydrator for 30 minutes. Strain through a fine-mesh strainer into a sterilized airtight jar or bottle. This will keep in a cool dark place for up to 1 week.

ASSEMBLY Arrange the cherry tomatoes on plates, with most having the center of the tomato facing up. The presentation should be natural—just quickly pour them on the plates and turn over a few that are facing down. Drizzle with basil oil, sprinkle with salt and pepper, and garnish with basil leaves and "Parmesan" shards. **SERVES 4**

golden tomato and lemon cucumber gazpacho with avocado salsa

Gazpacho is one of my favorite summer meals—I love not only the texture and flavor contrasts but also the ease of preparation. On a beautiful warm evening, I'm often in the mood for something that can be quickly prepared. With a blender and some really fresh ingredients, this dish can be made in five minutes. Gazpacho is best served chilled, with an equally cool glass of white wine.

GAZPACHO
2 cups peeled, deseeded, and diced lemon cucumbers
2 cups deseeded and diced tomatillos
2^1/$_4$ cups diced golden tomatoes
2 tablespoons lime juice
^{1}/$_2$ jalapeño pepper
Salt to taste
2 tablespoons olive oil

AVOCADO SALSA
1 avocado, diced
1 tablespoon chopped cilantro
1 teaspoon minced jalapeño
1 teaspoon lime juice
Salt and pepper to taste

GARNISH
Olive oil
Black pepper

GAZPACHO Mix all ingredients except olive oil in a large bowl; season to taste. Place ¾ of mixture in a food processor and process until smooth. Add back to bowl and stir to combine.

AVOCADO SALSA Combine all ingredients.

ASSEMBLY Serve chilled with avocado salsa, a few drops of olive oil, and freshly ground pepper. SERVES 4

apricots with star anise syrup and crumble

With raw food, as with all cooking, we often make things as complex as possible before we simplify them. In my early days with this food, I was always searching for a magical pastry recipe for desserts; but these days, especially in the summer, I like to focus on retaining the fruits' natural texture and flavor while subtly enhancing it. This dish could not be simpler to prepare and is easily adapted to peaches, nectarines, or any other stone fruit.

Apricots were first discovered growing in the wild on mountainsides in China and were brought to California by the Spanish, where 95 percent of the U.S. apricots are now grown. Although our harvest on the East Coast is limited, for the few weeks we have apricots, they are delicious and abundant at farmers markets.

APRICOTS
16 apricots
$3/4$ cup raw agave

CRUMBLE
$2^1/2$ cups cashew flour
$1^1/4$ cups oat flour
6 tablespoons water

$3/4$ cup plus 2 tablespoons maple syrup
1 tablespoon vanilla extract
$1^1/2$ teaspoons sea salt
1 tablespoon cinnamon

SYRUP
1 cup raw agave
$1/2$ teaspoon ground star anise
2 tablespoons lemon juice

APRICOTS Cut apricots in half and discard stones. Toss fruit with agave. Place on dehydrator screens and dehydrate 20–30 minutes.

CRUMBLE Mix ingredients in a medium-size bowl by hand. Spread flat on dehydrator screens. Dehydrate 8–10 hours until dry; crumble by hand and place back in dehydrator.

Dehydrate overnight. Process in a food processor into crumbs.

SYRUP Blend ingredients in a Vita-Mix to combine.

ASSEMBLY Place 8 apricot halves on each plate. Sprinkle top with crumbs just before serving. Spoon syrup over each serving. SERVES 4

beet ravioli with fava bean purée and green herb oil

When most people think of a beet, they are considering the standard red beet—there is nothing wrong with that, or the phrase "beet red," but I love beets for their versatility in the same way that I love tomatoes and plums for their many varieties, tastes, and textures. In the summer, when golden, white, red, candy stripe, and other varieties are available directly from the garden, they are good in many raw food preparations. Given that root vegetables are rather fibrous, they are best when sliced thin, minced, or otherwise broken down in such a way to easily consume—and they also taste better this way. I like using them as a carpaccio or, in this recipe, preparing them like a carpaccio and using them as the outside of a ravioli. The day I prepared this dish, it was late August in Maine and fava beans were still in season. With a little olive oil, they were lightly warmed, making a very sweet, nutty purée that was a good counterbalance to the crunch of beet, not to mention a very colorful combination.

BEETS
10 medium-size varietal beets (candy stripe, white, golden, red)
$1/4$ cup olive oil
3 tablespoons lime juice
1 tablespoon raw agave

PURÉE
$1^1/2$ pounds shelled fava beans
$1/4$ cup olive oil
2 tablespoons lemon juice
$1/2$ teaspoon salt

2 tablespoons chopped fresh mint
1 tablespoon nutritional yeast
2 tablespoons chopped fresh basil

OIL
1 cup fresh green herb leaves (mint, basil, oregano, parsley)
1 cup pure olive oil

GARNISH
Fresh summer herbs

BEETS Peel the beets and trim the edges to make them square. Slice very thin on a mandolin, keeping each type of beet separate. Combine the remaining ingredients and lightly brush the beet slices.

PURÉE Peel and rinse fava beans. Combine with olive oil and warm in a dehydrator for 90 minutes. Process until smooth with remaining ingredients.

OIL Place herb leaves in a blender with the olive oil. Purée until smooth. Place in a bowl or low-sided pan and put into dehydrator for 30 minutes. Strain through a fine-mesh strainer into a sterilized airtight jar or bottle. This will keep in a cool dark place for up to 1 week.

ASSEMBLY Prepare a "sandwich" of the beets by placing 1 tablespoon fava purée on $1/2$ of the slices. Top with the other slice and lightly press together, but not so much that the purée comes past the sides. On each plate, place 1 of each type of "ravioli," and on each plate, at least one duplicate. There should be 5–6 on each plate. Drizzle with herb oil and garnish with fresh herbs. **SERVES 4**

plum carpaccio with vanilla-agave syrup and ginger cream

This carpaccio may be the prettiest dish I have ever worked with. One day, I came back from the Greenmarket with the most beautiful plums but had no idea what to do with them; it soon became apparent that I needed to keep them as whole as possible. I made a quick vanilla syrup with agave and sliced the plums thin enough to have a bit of translucency to them but thick enough to have a little crunch.

CARPACCIO
4 red plums
4 yellow plums
4 blue plums
4 purple plums

SYRUP
1 cup raw agave
1 vanilla bean, scraped

CREAM
1 cup cashews, soaked 1–2 hours
1/2 cup water
2 tablespoons ginger juice
1 tablespoon raw agave
Pinch sea salt

GARNISH
Lavender sprigs

SYRUP Combine ingredients and mix well.

CREAM Blend all ingredients in a Vita-Mix until smooth. Keep cool.

ASSEMBLY Wash the plums, halve them, remove pits, and slice very thin using a mandolin or sharp knife. Place the plum slices on each plate, alternating the colors. Just before serving, pour enough syrup over just to coat. This dish is going to take you 10 minutes to make. Slicing the plums close to when they are being served is recommended. Garnish with a scoop of cream and lavender sprigs.
SERVES 4

raspberry parfait, vanilla bean cream, dark chocolate sauce, and coconut brittle

Some dishes are simply crowd-pleasers, combining a number of components and ingredients that have mass appeal. I love inventive combinations and textures, but I must admit, if I could eat one dessert only, it might be this. It's easy to love and easy to adapt to different fruits, flavored creams, and any number of crunch additions such as spiced macadamia nuts, candied almonds, or whatever you desire.

BRITTLE
1 cup dried coconut
1 cup macadamia nuts, dehydrated overnight and chopped
1/3 cup maple syrup powder
1/4 cup maple syrup
1 tablespoon ground ginger

CREAM
2 cups young coconut meat
1/4 cup raw agave
1/2 vanilla bean, scraped
2 tablespoons lemon juice
2 tablespoons melted coconut oil
1/4 teaspoon sea salt

SAUCE
1 1/2 cups cacao nibs
1 1/4 cups raw agave
1/2 cup coconut oil
1 cup maple syrup
1 tablespoon vanilla extract
Pinch sea salt

GARNISH
1 quart raspberries
Fresh mint leaves, optional

BRITTLE Process all ingredients in a food processor just until combined. Spread into a thin, uneven layer on Teflex dehydrator sheets and dehydrate 8–10 hours. Turn onto screens and dehydrate overnight. Break apart into small pieces and dehydrate another 6–8 hours.

CREAM Blend all ingredients in a Vita-Mix until completely smooth. Chill before serving.

SAUCE Blend all ingredients in Vita-Mix until completely smooth.

ASSEMBLY Warm chocolate sauce slightly in dehydrator. Place about 1/2 inch of chocolate sauce at the bottom of a martini or stemmed cocktail glass. Add a layer of raspberries, then a layer of cream, sprinkle with brittle, and repeat until there are three layers of each. Finish with a final layer of chocolate. Top the parfait with raspberries and mint leaves. **SERVES 4**

green tomato–"ricotta" tart with basil "ice cream"

It's not as strange as it may sound—by now, we all know that tomatoes are a fruit, despite their status as a vegetable in most dishes. They may not be standard fare for a dessert, but this is really a slightly sweetened variation of classical flavors.

TART

CRUST
2 cups nut flour (see recipe below)
$1/4$ teaspoon salt
2 tablespoons maple syrup
1 tablespoon coconut oil
1 tablespoon date paste

NUT FLOUR
2 cups walnut halves
2 cups pecan halves
2 cups almonds
$1/3$ cup plus 1 tablespoon maple syrup
1 teaspoon vanilla extract
$1/2$ tablespoon sea salt
$1 1/2$ tablespoons ground cinnamon
$1 1/2$ cups maple powder

"RICOTTA"
$1 1/4$ cups cashews, soaked 1–2 hours
$1/4$ cup coconut meat

2 tablespoons lemon juice
$1/4$ cup plus 2 tablespoons raw agave
$1/4$ cup plus 2 tablespoons melted coconut oil
$1/4$ cup water
$1/2$ teaspoon vanilla extract
$1/4$ teaspoon sea salt
$1/2$ vanilla bean, scraped

CONFIT
8 unripe green tomatoes, seeded and diced
$1/2$ cup raw agave
$1/4$ teaspoon salt

"ICE CREAM"
1 cup cashews, soaked 1–2 hours
$1/2$ cup coconut meat
$1/2$ cup raw agave
$1 1/4$ cups water
Pinch sea salt
$1/2$ cup coconut oil
$1/2$ cup basil

CRUST Mix all ingredients together well by hand. Line 1 tart shell with plastic wrap. Press dough very thin into tart shell. Dehydrate 48 hours. Chill crust in freezer for 15–30 minutes before filling.

NUT FLOUR Soak nuts overnight; drain. Dehydrate 24 hours. In a large bowl, coat dehydrated nuts with maple syrup. Combine vanilla, salt, cinnamon, and maple powder, and stir into nuts until they are well coated. Dehydrate on screens for 48 hours. Grind to flour in a food processor.

"RICOTTA" Blend all ingredients in a Vita-Mix until very smooth. Fill candied nut crust and chill in freezer overnight. Remove pie from metal tart shell and wrap in plastic wrap. Store in freezer.

CONFIT Toss tomatoes with agave and salt. Dehydrate 30–45 minutes on Teflex sheets. Reserve.

"ICE CREAM" Blend all ingredients until smooth. Pour into ice cream maker and follow manufacturer's instructions.

ASSEMBLY Cut tart into 8–10 slices with a sharp knife. Optional: You can make 4 small tart shells instead of 1 large. Store any extra crust in quart containers in the freezer.

Spread the green tomato confit across the tart and garnish with "ice cream." **SERVES 4**

Although nature commences
with reason and ends in
experience it is necessary
for us to do the opposite, that is to
commence with experience and from
this to proceed to investigate the reason.

—Leonardo Da Vinci

contemporary

You've probably already guessed that contemporary would be my favorite chapter. What most interests me about food is the relationship between time, history, experience—and taste. The spatial differences are profound in some cases, and I was fortunate to learn this early in my career. On a trip to Morocco many years ago, I was taken to a very traditional restaurant in the Medina of Marrakesh, a place where time seems to have stopped and the narrow streets are paved with history and tradition. Upon entering Yacout through a massive old wooden door, you are transported into a magical world of sensory feelings: the feeling of warmth, the smell of spice, the glow of lanterns, the silence of greenery, and the pull of seduction placed on all diners. It is, for the most part, indescribable; but many, including me, will try to convey the experience in words.

It was there that I first tasted the famous Moroccan Lemon Chicken, which is known for its distinct flavor of salty preserved lemon, green olives, and ginger. The chicken was cooked like a stew, with bones, and in a sauce rich with onion, saffron, ginger, and hot pepper. It is a haunting flavor that one can never forget. I left Morocco after that visit with an eagerness that I will always seek to replenish—the desire to be in a kitchen and apply my own set of culinary skills—armed with my newly acquired taste memories.

Back in New York, one of the city's most esteemed chefs, Jean-Georges Vongrichten, was in the process of opening his first restaurant as an owner, called JoJo, on Manhattan's Upper East Side. Jean-Georges is known for his wildly inventive use of infused oils and juices, all rooted in traditional cooking, and I was very excited to try his new restaurant. I was there on opening night and dozens of times in the next two years. On one of my early visits, I ordered a dish simply described as Chicken (with olives, lemon, and chickpea fries). It sounded simple enough and looked very light and clean—a very contemporary presentation like many other New York dishes at the time. And then, one bite, the flavors exploded, and I was taken back to Yacout—but this was New York. What was happening? I discovered, eventually, what more seasoned chefs already had. Flavors, feelings, moods, and ideas were transportable. The higher-end chefs were not simply cooks; they were artists, inspired by real-life experience and emotion. In the beginning, as in any art, it appears that replication may be taking place, but the reality is that inspiration may appear in a variety of forms. In this case, it was clear that Jean-Georges had probably shared a similar experience to mine and applied that to his own brand of cuisine. He found an avenue to reapply experience—in this case, taste memory—into his art.

With raw food, outside influences are very important. With a short history of culinary imagination, the cuisine is still in its infancy. In order for it to reach its highest potential, it is necessary to connect with individuals on an emotional and physical level, and then, on a more basic note, as a chef. I'd like to point out that the preparation of raw food is so new that I can't think of a better canvas for creative food.

When I initially became involved in raw food, my early influences were traditional dishes that were well known: lasagna, ravioli, pasta, and so forth. Over the past couple of years, my style has evolved well beyond that, and I now find that the most interesting cuisine is based on life—or art that represents life experience. Whether it is film, sculpture, architecture, or music, I believe that the path to the highest level of this cuisine is through its relationship to art; and for that reason, much of my food is influenced by it. The best dishes have come from this concept—the inspiration may be the Rolling Stones, Salvador Dali, or *The Wizard of Oz*. The importance of a connection to deeper meaning is paramount. Often, the concept is simpler, such as a black-and-white dinner that I once did: foods that were black and white and nothing more. The important element is to push the boundaries, find the core, and, ultimately, provide a great experience for guests.

hijiki and kohlrabi with sweet tahini dressing

Hijiki is extremely easy to work with, and this recipe can be prepared in a few minutes. Since the vegetables remain crisper and brighter when freshly cut, it is best made just before serving. I find that hijiki is suited to a creamy dressing, and the texture and nutty flavor of tahini is well matched in this dish, providing a simple but interesting contrast of black and white.

HIJIKI
3 cups hijiki seaweed
1 kohlrabi, peeled, thinly sliced, and cut into desired shapes

DRESSING
$^1/_2$ cup raw agave
$^2/_3$ cup tahini
$^1/_4$ cup water

$^1/_3$ cup miso
2 tablespoons lemon juice
Salt

GARNISH
Salt and pepper to taste
Chives, cut in 1-inch lengths
White sesame seeds

HIJIKI Soak hijiki in warm water 20–30 minutes and drain.

DRESSING Blend all ingredients in a Vita-Mix.

ASSEMBLY Dress the hijiki and $^2/_3$ of the kohlrabi with just enough dressing to coat lightly. Season with salt and pepper. Pour a pool of dressing on plates and top with hijiki. Garnish with kohlrabi, chives, and sesame seeds. SERVES 4–6

black-and-white tofu, trumpet mushroom salad, sesame enoki mushrooms, white asparagus, and miso broth

Often, in the pursuit of art, I purposely work within concepts that apply narrow limitations. The results, like the movements of a contortionist, are always interesting. The purpose of this exploration is not solely to be creative or different but to better understand the possibilities within the cuisine. The black-and-white menu was one of the most challenging menus I've done, and I learned a great deal from it, including how to prepare this tasty and dramatic recipe.

WHITE TOFU
1 cup cashews, soaked 1–2 hours
$1/2$ cup fresh young Thai coconut meat
$1/2$ cup raw carageenan
$1/2$ cup water
$1/4$ teaspoon sea salt

BLACK TOFU
1 cup cashews, soaked 1–2 hours
$1/2$ cup fresh young Thai coconut meat
$1/2$ cup raw carrageenan
$1/4$ cup water
$1/4$ cup ground black sesame paste
$1/4$ teaspoon sea salt

MUSHROOMS
1 cup enoki mushrooms
2 tablespoons sesame oil
1 teaspoon nama shoyu
Pinch sea salt

SALAD
1 cup black trumpet mushrooms
1 tablespoon white miso
1 teaspoon minced fresh ginger
1 tablespoon sesame oil
1 tablespoon lemon juice
1 tablespoon raw agave

ASPARAGUS
1 small bunch asparagus
2 tablespoons olive oil
Pinch salt

BROTH
1 cup water
$1/2$ cup nama shoyu
2 tablespoons dried dulse
1 tablespoon wakame
$1/4$ cup miso paste

WHITE TOFU Line the bottom and sides of a small pan or square container with plastic wrap. Drain cashews. Blend all ingredients in a Vita-Mix until completely smooth. Pour into lined pan, then cover with plastic wrap. (Tofu should be about $1\frac{1}{2}$ inches thick.) Refrigerate about 2 hours until firm. When ready to serve, remove tofu from container by lifting plastic wrap out of pan and gently transferring tofu to a cutting board. Cut tofu into 2-inch squares with a butter knife. Repeat this same procedure for black tofu.

MUSHROOMS Combine all ingredients and allow mushrooms to marinate for at least 1 hour.

SALAD Toss mushrooms with remaining ingredients; spread on Teflex sheets and dehydrate 20–30 minutes.

ASPARAGUS Cut white asparagus into 1-inch lengths on a bias and toss just to coat with olive oil and season with salt; dehydrate 45 minutes.

BROTH Combine all ingredients. Place in a dehydrator for 90 minutes. Strain and reserve.

ASSEMBLY On a large, preferably high-rimmed plate, set two pieces of tofu, one of each color (the plates can alternate which have two of each). Garnish the white tofu with salad; garnish the black tofu with mushrooms. Pour enough broth into each bowl to come up to $1/4$ of the tofu's height and place a few asparagus spears inside the broth.
SERVES 4

black sesame and white coconut dumplings with creamy miso sauce

These dumplings are perhaps the most stunning dish I have ever served—they are ultra simple and elegant, like a black-tie affair, but the concept is undeniably charming and sophisticated. Fortunately, they taste even better than they look and have became an instant classic of mine.

BLACK SESAME DUMPLINGS

2 cups young coconut meat
$^1/_3$ cup black sesame tahini
$^1/_4$ teaspoon salt

WHITE COCONUT DUMPLINGS

2 cups young coconut meat
$^1/_4$ teaspoon salt

FILLING

4 cups cashews, soaked 1–2 hours
4 tablespoons sesame oil
2 teaspoons salt
4 tablespoons nama shoyu
4 tablespoons minced scallions
4 tablespoons minced fresh ginger

MISO SAUCE

$^1/_2$ cup cashews, soaked 1–2 hours
$^1/_3$ cup tahini
$^1/_4$ cup white miso
$^1/_4$ cup nama shoyu
$^1/_4$ cup packed dulse
$^1/_4$ cup raw agave
$^1/_4$ cup ginger juice

GARNISH

Chives
2 tablespoons chopped scallions
$^1/_4$ cup black sesame tahini

BLACK SESAME DUMPLINGS Blend ingredients in a Vita-Mix until smooth. Spread very thin on dehydrator Teflex sheets and dehydrate 3–4 hours. Remove from Teflex and invert onto a cutting board. Trim edges evenly. Cut into 9 squares. Repeat this same procedure for the white coconut dumplings.

FILLING In a food processor, pulse the cashews until coarsely minced. In a separate bowl, combine cashews with remaining ingredients.

MISO SAUCE Blend all ingredients in Vita-Mix until smooth.

ASSEMBLY To prepare the wrappers, brush one side of the white wrapper with water and lay a black wrapper across it diagonally so that there are 8 points. Brush with water and place 1 tablespoon filling in the center. Pull the outsides together so that the dumplings bunch together like a sack. Tie a chive around each to secure.

On each plate, pour 3 tablespoons sauce in the center and spread gently with a spoon, being careful not to let sauce go to the edges of the plate. Place 2 dumplings on each plate, and drop just a few drops of black sesame tahini on the plate. YIELDS 16

"paul smith" basil and young spinach-striped flan with white cardamom foam and lemon dust

Paul Smith is known for his use of colorful stripes in fashion (so many other designers attempt to use these patterns without the same elegance); his designs are understated yet bold in their essence. This flan was almost an impossible production to put together but well worth the effort once we developed this method.

FLAN

BASIL MOUSSE
1 cup cashews, soaked 1–2 hours
1/2 cup fresh young Thai coconut meat
1/2 cup raw carrageenan
1/4 cup water
1/4 cup ground sesame paste
1/4 cup chopped fresh basil
1/4 teaspoon sea salt

SPINACH MOUSSE
1 cup cashews, soaked 1–2 hours
1/2 cup fresh young Thai coconut meat

1/2 cup raw carrageenan
1/4 cup water
1/4 cup ground sesame paste
1/4 cup spinach juice
1/4 teaspoon sea salt

LEMON DUST
Zest of 2 lemons

FOAM
2 cups water
1 cup brazil nuts, soaked 6 hours
1 tablespoon white cardamom powder
1 tablespoon salt

BASIL MOUSSE Blend all ingredients in a Vita-Mix until very smooth. Reserve. Repeat this same procedure for the spinach mousse.

FLAN ASSEMBLY Line 6 flan molds tightly with plastic wrap. Pour 1/4 inch of basil mousse into flan mold, followed by 1/4 inch of spinach mousse. Alternate to the top of flan mold and cover tightly with plastic wrap. Refrigerate at least 4 hours until firm. When ready to serve, remove flan from mold by lifting plastic wrap out of mold and gently transferring to a plate.

LEMON DUST Finally chop zest and dehydrate overnight. Pulverize in a mortar and pestle or food processor.

FOAM Blend all ingredients in Vita-Mix until smooth. Strain and place back in blender.

ASSEMBLY Place one flan on each plate and gently cut it down the center from top to bottom. Turn one of the halves 45 degrees so that its point touches the center of the other half. This is to better show the layers. For the foam, turn Vita-Mix on its highest speed for one minute. Spoon foam from top of blender with a tablespoon and place around flan. Sprinkle with lemon dust. **SERVES 4–6**

rothko terrine and grapefruit-infused jicama "rice"

It was fitting that Rothko was the inspiration for the first course of our contemporary art dinner. Rothko's attention to color, shape, balance, and depth was responsible for some of the most unique yet widely recognized art of his time. Artists inspire our work not only with their original perspective and expression but also with their ability to capture the hearts of a public with enormously diverse methods of understanding. There is much to be learned from the work of a unique impossible-to-copy artist whose work has inspired many.

The Myth holds us, therefore, not through its romantic flavor, not the remembrance of beauty of some bygone age, not through the possibilities of fantasy, but because it expresses to us something real and existing in ourselves, as it was to those who first stumbled upon the symbols to give them life. — *Mark Rothko*

TERRINE

BEET LAYER
Salt
Black pepper
2 red beets, peeled and finely minced
1/4 cup Irish moss
1/4 cup olive oil
1/2 cup vegetable stock (cucumber and celery juice with salt, pepper, rosemary, and thyme)

MANGO LAYER
2 cups frozen mango purée
Pinch salt
1/4 teaspoon cayenne pepper

1 tablespoon fresh lime juice
1 fresh mango, peeled and cut into thin 1-inch slices

AVOCADO LAYER
2 avocados, sliced
1/4 cup Irish moss
1/2 teaspoon salt
Pinch black pepper
1 tablespoon fresh lime juice

"RICE"
3 cups chopped jicama
1 cup macadamia nuts
1 teaspoon sea salt
1/2 cup fresh grapefruit juice
1 tablespoon raw agave

BEET LAYER Mix together dry ingredients in a large bowl. Add remaining ingredients; mix well with hands. Line 2 half sheet pans with parchment. Gently press in 2 pans; smooth into 1½-inch even layers. Dehydrate in bottom of dehydrators 6–8 hours. Flip onto cutting board and trim edges. Place on screens. Dehydrate another 3–4 hours. Carefully cut pieces to fit the entire bottom of a plastic-lined terrine mold. Refrigerate.

MANGO LAYER Blend ingredients in a Vita-Mix until very smooth; freeze. Spread a 1¼-inch layer on top of the beet in terrine mold and freeze entire terrine.

AVOCADO LAYER Blend all ingredients until smooth. Spread a 1-inch layer on top of mango and refrigerate.

"RICE" Process jicama and macadamia nuts in a food processor until a rice-like consistency is achieved. Dry mixture between paper towels or strain through cheesecloth to remove excess moisture. In a medium bowl, combine sea salt, grapefruit juice, and agave. Add rice mixture and toss until well combined. Spread mixture on Teflex sheets and dehydrate 1–2 hours to remove excess moisture.

ASSEMBLY Carefully unmold terrine and slice into 1¼- to 1½-inch slices. Serve on top of molded square of rice.
SERVES 4–6

portobello "foie gras" on sun-dried tomato flatbread

In truth, I don't support *foie gras* production in any way, but as a verbal significance, *foie gras* means ultra rich and decadent. Since it will likely or hopefully be banned in its original incarnation in the near future, there will be many interpretations of the classic. Portobello mushrooms are meaty and are a great way to introduce skeptics to the possibilities within raw cuisine.

"FOIE GRAS"

4 portobello mushrooms, chopped, brushed with olive oil, salt and pepper, and dehydrated 2 hours
1 cup olive oil
1/2 cup Irish moss carrageenan
Salt

FLATBREAD

1 cup flax meal
1/2 cup well-chopped sun-dried tomatoes
1 1/2 cups walnuts, soaked 8–10 hours
2 yellow squash, chopped

1 teaspoon salt
1/4 teaspoon black pepper
1/4 cup olive oil
1/2 teaspoon chili powder

GARNISH

2 tablespoons truffle oil
Sea salt
2 tablespoons chopped parsley

"FOIE GRAS" Blend all ingredients in a Vita-Mix until smooth. Spread at least 1 inch thick in a plastic-lined loaf or terrine pan and refrigerate until firm.

FLATBREAD Place flax meal and sun-dried tomatoes in a medium-size bowl; set aside. Blend remaining ingredients in a Vita-Mix until smooth. Add to flax meal and sun-dried tomatoes, and combine well. Spread 1/3 inch thick on Teflex sheets and dehydrate 8–10 hours. Transfer bread to screens, cut into 2 x 3-inch rectangles, and dehydrate 4–6 hours.

ASSEMBLY Serve foie gras on flatbread. Drizzle with a touch of truffle oil and sprinkle with coarse sea salt and parsley. SERVES 4

jackson pollock raviolo with arugula pesto

I've rarely had such a good time plating a dish as I did this raviolo. The coconut wrappers have become so versatile in my repertoire that the "pasta" itself was easy, especially having so many great fruit and vegetable juices to work with. But the real fun was "splattering" the plates (and the floors and clothes) with the pesto. Although this is a very serious and advanced dish, in its own subtle way, the concept of letting loose a little is a nice reminder that food preparation need not be rigid and limited. In fact, taking risks and expanding our methods will often lead to intriguing results.

It doesn't make much difference how the paint is put on as long as something has been said. Technique is just a means of arriving at a statement. *—Jackson Pollock*

RAVIOLO

WRAPPERS
4 cups young Thai coconut
1 teaspoon salt
$1/4$ cup frozen mango purée
$1/4$ cup blended and strained red pepper purée
$1/4$ cup spinach juice

FILLING
$3^1/2$ cups Brazil nuts, soaked 2–3 hours
$1/4$ cup fresh lemon juice
$1/2$ cup water

1 cup olive oil
$1^1/2$ teaspoons salt
2 teaspoons nutritional yeast

PESTO
2 cups packed arugula
1 cup packed mint
1 cup packed parsley
$1/4$ cup pine nuts
1 teaspoon salt
Black pepper
$1/2$ cup olive oil

WRAPPERS Blend coconut and salt in a Vita-Mix until very smooth. Spread thin on Teflex dehydrator sheets and dehydrate 1 hour. Pull out sheets and splatter coconut wrappers with purées and spinach juice. Dehydrate another $2^1/2$ to 3 hours. Remove colored sheets from Teflex, trim edges, and cut into 6 rectangular pieces.

FILLING Process all ingredients in a food processor 3–5 minutes until smooth.

PESTO Process all ingredients except olive oil in food processor until combined and chunky. With machine running, add olive oil. Check seasoning.

ASSEMBLY Place 1 tablespoon raviolo filling just off center of each pasta sheet—fold over to make corners meet, press edges together, and flatten a bit by hand. Place two raviolo on each plate and splatter plate with pesto. SERVES 4–6

cubist mushrooms and white asparagus with red pepper curry sauce and black sesame crackers

I've always been a fan of Picasso and have read numerous books about his work and life. I am especially enamored of his ability to work in many different mediums throughout his career, always with success. The Cubist period was so inventive, so unique, that it will always be respected in the art world. Morel mushrooms reminded me of an earlier work of his, and that fact, along with the presence of other earth tones, gave this dish its title.

ASPARAGUS
8 spears white asparagus
3 tablespoons olive oil
$1/4$ teaspoon salt
$1/4$ teaspoon black pepper
2 sprigs thyme
2 sprigs rosemary

MUSHROOMS
MORELS
12 morels, soaked in water and rinsed 2–3 times
3 tablespoons olive oil
$1/4$ teaspoon salt
Black pepper
$1^1/2$ cups vegetable stock (see page 64)

ALMOND MUSHROOMS
4 almond mushrooms, lightly brushed
3 tablespoons olive oil
$1/4$ teaspoon salt
Black pepper

ENOKI MUSHROOMS
1 cup enoki mushrooms
2 tablespoons olive oil
Pinch salt

CURRY SAUCE
$1^1/2$ cups puréed and strained red bell pepper
2 cups cubed mango
$1/2$ teaspoon salt
Pinch cayenne pepper
2 tablespoons curry powder

CRACKERS
2 cups black sesame seeds
1 cup flax meal
3 Roma tomatoes
$1^1/2$ teaspoons salt
$3/4$ teaspoon cumin
$1/4$ cup water
Pinch cayenne

ASPARAGUS Cut asparagus on a bias into $1^1/2$-inch lengths. Toss with remaining ingredients; spread out in a shallow pan. Let "poach" in dehydrator at 115 degrees F for 4–6 hours, or until asparagus pieces are tender.

MORELS Cut morels lengthwise in half or in thirds. Toss with olive oil, salt, and pepper. Place on dehydrator Teflex sheets and dehydrate 1–2 hours. Spread in a shallow pan and pour in vegetable stock. Cover pan in plastic wrap and place in bottom of dehydrator for 3–4 hours at 115 degrees F.

ALMOND MUSHROOMS Cut almond mushrooms into eighths. Toss with olive oil, salt, and pepper. Place on dehydrator Teflex sheets and dehydrate 1–2 hours.

ENOKI MUSHROOMS Trim 1 inch from base of mushrooms and discard; place trimmed mushrooms in a bowl. Toss with olive oil and salt. Cover bowl and reserve.

CURRY SAUCE Blend all ingredients in a Vita-Mix.

CRACKERS Place black sesame seeds and flax meal in a bowl and set aside. Blend remaining ingredients in Vita-Mix until smooth and pour into a bowl. Mix with sesame seeds and flax meal until well combined. Spread thinly on Teflex sheets and score into desired shape. Dehydrate until crisp.

ASSEMBLY Pour a generous amount of sauce on plates to cover bottoms—intersperse mushrooms and asparagus very freely on plate. Garnish with crackers. **SERVES 4–6**

shiitake ravioli with broccoli rabe, balsamic fig purée, and ginger cream

Around the time I began working with raw foods, I was also practicing a lot of yoga, about two hours each day in the early afternoon. As I grew more comfortable in my postures, my mind began to expand; and after the sessions, I did my best thinking. I was pressed for a new dish for a potential magazine article about what I was working on and, with very little practical experience with this cuisine, a variation of this dish appeared in my imagination. In execution, it was exactly as I had envisioned, along with a substantial amount of extra labor that I did not plan for. The concept is one that can be applied to many different dishes—simply by changing the vegetable or modifying the sauce with different spices. For example, a bok choy, sesame, and ginger filling with a curry cream would be excellent.

WRAPPERS
4 young Thai coconuts

FILLING AND RABE
2 cups shiitake mushrooms, quartered
$1/4$ cup olive oil, divided
Salt
Pepper
2 cups broccoli rabe, cut into 2-inch lengths

PURÉE
6 dried figs
1 cup balsamic vinegar
2 tablespoons raw agave nectar
$1/4$ teaspoon ground anise seed

CREAM
1 cup cashews, soaked 1–2 hours
1 cup reserved coconut water
3 tablespoons ginger juice
1 tablespoon raw agave
Sea salt

WRAPPERS Open coconuts; strain water and reserve. Chop top off coconut, just where it begins to turn inward. Carefully remove the coconut meat using the back of a spoon, keeping the bottom in 1 piece and the top in 1 piece. Cut coconut into 2-inch squares, and then, very carefully, slice each in half the long way, making several very thin pasta squares.

FILLING AND RABE Toss mushrooms in a bowl with half the olive oil, and season with salt and pepper. Spread on Teflex sheets and dehydrate 45 minutes. Toss the broccoli rabe with remaining olive oil, season with salt and pepper, and dehydrate 1 hour.

PURÉE Blend all ingredients in a Vita-Mix until smooth.

CREAM Blend all ingredients in Vita-Mix until smooth.

ASSEMBLY Dip each pasta square in the ginger cream and place 4 on each plate. Add broccoli rabe and $2/3$ of the mushrooms to top each square. Top with another pasta square, then remaining mushrooms. Drizzle sauce around raviolis and fig sauce over the tops. **SERVES 4**

green tea canneloni, banana lemongrass cream, almond "gelato," and goji lime sauce

One of my earliest experiments was a Japanese dinner, where we pushed the boundaries with a number of new dishes. I recall writing the menu and wondering how in the world we would actually make this dish. Kristen, one of the sous chefs, did an amazing job by fulfilling the vision and creating one of the most sophisticated desserts to come out of my kitchen.

CANNELONI
2 1/2 cups oat flour
1 1/2 cups cashew flour
1/4 teaspoon salt
2 tablespoons raw agave
1/2 teaspoon vanilla extract
1/2 cup maple syrup
2 1/2 tablespoons green tea powder

CREAM
1 1/2 cups cashews, soaked 1–2 hours
1 1/2 ripe bananas
1/2 cup coconut meat
1/4 cup lemongrass juice
1/2 teaspoon salt
1 vanilla bean, scraped
1 tablespoon fresh lemon juice
2 tablespoons water
1/4 cup raw agave
1/4 cup coconut oil

"GELATO"
1/2 cup cashews, soaked 1–2 hours
1 cup macadamia nuts, soaked 1–2 hours
1/4 cup coconut meat
3/4 cup raw agave
1 cup water
2 teaspoons vanilla extract
1 tablespoon almond extract
Pinch sea salt
1/2 cup coconut oil

LIME SAUCE
1/4 cup goji berries, soaked 15 minutes and strained
1/4 cup raw agave
1/2 cup lime juice
1 tablespoon lime zest

CANNELONI Using your hands, mix ingredients until well combined. Roll thin and cut with a ring mold; wrap around a cylinder to shape canneloni. Dehydrate 48 hours.

CREAM Blend all ingredients in a Vita-Mix until smooth.

"GELATO" Blend all ingredients in Vita-Mix until smooth.

LIME SAUCE Blend all ingredients in Vita-Mix until smooth.

ASSEMBLY Fill each canneloni with cream. Place a pool of lime sauce on each plate and set canneloni on sauce. Scoop "gelato" close to canneloni. SERVES 4

ocean vegetables and squash noodles with oyster-mushroom escabeche, faded green caviar, and miso tahini sauce

Sea vegetables are simply incredible—the flavors are all unique, as are the textures—and they harbor some of the most important nutrients we ever need. For a vegan, it becomes even more important to find tasty sources of these minerals, and these are the best. Now that they have become mainstream, it is quite possible to build elaborate flavors and presentations around them.

VEGETABLES
4 ounces pink seaweed (tosaka), washed and soaked overnight
4 ounces wakame, reconstituted
4 ounces hijiki, reconstituted
4 ounces kelp, reconstituted
4 ounces light green seaweed (ogonori), washed and soaked overnight
4 ounces arame, reconstituted
Black and white sesame seeds
1 small knob fresh ginger, cut into very thin batons
1 medium beet, cut into very thin batons
1 small carrot, cut into very thin batons
1 small zucchini, cut into thin spirals
1 small jicama, peeled and cut into very thin batons

NOODLES
1 yellow squash, cut into long noodles with a spiralizer
Salt
Olive oil

ESCABECHE
$1/2$ cup olive oil
$1/4$ cup apple cider vinegar
1 teaspoon ground mustard
1 tablespoon dried oregano
1 teaspoon salt
1 teaspoon black pepper
8 ounces oyster mushrooms

CAVIAR
6 ounces arame
$1/2$ cup Irish moss
$1/4$ cup water
3 tablespoons spinach juice
Pinch salt

SAUCE
$1^1/2$ cups raw agave
2 cups tahini
$1^1/2$ cups water
$1^1/4$ cups miso
$1/4$ cup lemon juice

GARNISH
Black and white sesame seeds

NOODLES Toss pasta with a bit of salt and olive oil. Form pasta into spiral bunches on Teflex sheets and dehydrate overnight. Transfer to a screen if needed and place another screen over spirals to keep in place; dehydrate an additional 24 hours.

ESCABECHE Blend all ingredients except mushrooms in a Vita-Mix and pour into a bowl. Add mushrooms, let marinate 15 minutes, then dehydrate on Teflex sheets for 20 minutes.

CAVIAR Soak the arame in warm water for 1 hour and drain. Blend all ingredients until very smooth and spread 1 inch thick onto a loaf pan. Refrigerate 4 hours. With the end of a small espresso spoon, lift out a very small (pearl-size) amount of the caviar. Spread these pearls onto a flat plate or pan.

SAUCE Blend ingredients in Vita-Mix.

ASSEMBLY Dress each of the sea vegetables separately with sauce. Dress each of the raw vegetables also with the sauce. Prepare individual large tablespoon-size piles of each sea vegetable in a serpent shape, with a different raw vegetable topped on each one. Alternate sprinkling them with black and white sesame seeds. On the arame, top with faded green caviar, and on the wakame, top with the crisp squash noodles. **SERVES 4**

gnocchi of broccoli rabe with ginger cream sauce, concord grape chutney, manchego paper, and dust of three leaves

The most alluring aspect of the New York Greenmarket in fall is the presence of Concord grapes—and their amazing juice—that a couple of farmers sell in Union Square. Bitter, sweet, salty, and sour are four sensations that, when properly combined, create the highest possible form of flavor. Broccoli rabe and Concord grapes really should be a classic combination!

BROCCOLI RABE GNOCCHI
1 cup chopped broccoli rabe
3 tablespoons olive oil
$1/2$ teaspoon salt
$1/4$ teaspoon black pepper
4 cups jicama, processed in food processor until finely pulsed and strained of excess water
2 cups cashews, soaked 1–2 hours
$1^1/2$ teaspoons sea salt
1 teaspoon nutritional yeast
$3/4$ cup fresh lemon juice
$1/2$ cup cashew flour

CHUTNEY
2 cups Concord grapes
2 cups seedless red grapes, diced small
1 teaspoon lime juice
Pinch freshly ground pepper
1 tablespoon minced ginger

SAUCE
1 cup cashews, soaked 1–2 hours
$3/4$ cup water
3 tablespoons ginger juice
2 tablespoons raw agave
$1/2$ teaspoon salt

MANCHEGO PAPER
4 cups coconut meat
$1/2$ teaspoon salt
3 tablespoons nutritional yeast
1 teaspoon fresh lemon juice

DUST OF THREE LEAVES
20 basil leaves
20 mint leaves
30 parsley leaves

BROCCOLI RABE GNOCCHI Marinate broccoli rabe in olive oil, salt, and pepper, then dehydrate 30 minutes.

Mix jicama, cashews, sea salt, nutritional yeast, lemon juice, and black pepper to taste in a large bowl. Blend in batches in a Vita-Mix until very smooth. Place all ingredients in a bowl and stir in cashew flour. Chop marinated and dehydrated broccoli rabe and gently stir into mixture by hand. Shape mixture into gnocchi and gently roll on screens to create a gnocchi pattern. Place in dehydrator for 2 hours until crust forms around outside. Serve immediately, or warm in dehydrator until ready to serve.

CHUTNEY Crush the Concord grapes through a strainer and reserve juice. In a food processor, pulse the grape juice, lime juice, pepper, ginger, and red grapes to combine, just a few seconds, but not to fully purée. Dehydrate in a shallow pan for 2 hours and let cool.

SAUCE Blend all ingredients in Vita-Mix until smooth.

MANCHEGO PAPER Blend all ingredients in Vita-Mix until completely smooth. Spread in a thin layer over dehydrator Teflex sheets. Dehydrate 4–5 hours, then break into large sheets.

DUST OF THREE LEAVES To make basil dust, place basil leaves between dehydrator screens. Dehydrate overnight or until crisp. Run through Vita-Mix to make into powder. Repeat process separately with mint and parsley leaves.

ASSEMBLY Sauce the gnocchi with enough ginger cream to lightly coat it. On one side, garnish with the grape chutney. Lay the manchego paper across the top and make three lines of herb dust across the top of that. SERVES 4

frozen pumpkin flan, cinnamon foam, and mandarin candy

Whenever I think of pumpkin, I can't help but remember the image of myself in a giant papier-mâché pumpkin that my dad made for me on Halloween many years ago. Ever since, it's been a lighthearted association. Interestingly enough, this dish is actually made with carrot, which provides the same starchiness, and the pumpkin spices supply the rest.

FLAN

FILLING

3 cups cashews, soaked 2–3 hours
$1/2$ cup maple syrup
$1/2$ cup raw agave
1 cup coconut oil
$1^1/4$ cups carrot juice
1 teaspoon vanilla
$1/2$ teaspoon salt
$1/4$ vanilla bean, scraped
3 teaspoons ground cinnamon
3 teaspoons ground nutmeg

CRUST

$2^1/2$ cups cashew flour
$1^3/4$ cups oat flour
$1/4$ cup water
$3/4$ cup maple syrup

1 tablespoon vanilla
$1^1/2$ teaspoons sea salt
1 tablespoon ground cinnamon
2 teaspoons ground nutmeg

FOAM

$1^1/2$ cups cashews, soaked 1–2 hours
3 cups water
2 teaspoons ground cinnamon
$1/4$ cup raw agave
$1/4$ cup coconut oil
1 vanilla bean, scraped

CANDY

3 cups coconut meat
1 cup fresh orange juice
$1/2$ teaspoon salt
$1/4$ cup maple syrup
$1/2$ cup orange zest

FILLING Blend all ingredients in a Vita-Mix until very smooth. Pour into plastic-lined ramekins and freeze.

CRUST Mix ingredients in a medium-size bowl by hand. Spread flat on dehydrator screens. Dehydrate at 115 degrees F for 4–5 hours until dry; crumble onto Teflex sheets. Dehydrate an additional 5 hours.

FOAM Blend cashews and water in Vita-Mix until smooth; strain through a fine chinois. Return cashew milk to Vita-Mix with remaining ingredients; blend until smooth. Use an immersion blender to create foam.

CANDY Blend all ingredients except zest in Vita-Mix until completely smooth. Spread in a $1/8$-inch-thick layer over dehydrator Teflex sheets and sprinkle zest over top. Dehydrate 4–5 hours, cut into strips, and carefully wrap around cylinders. Dehydrate until crisp.

ASSEMBLY Using a square or round ring mold, press $1/4$ inch of the crust into the bottom of the mold and top with the flan. Remove mold and drizzle foam around edges. Top with mandarin candy. SERVES 4

end-of-season heirloom tomatoes,
warm "cheese" crisps, and melting
olive oil "ice cream"

Occasionally, the purpose of food is to awaken the palette, tease the mind, and provide entertainment while nourishing at the same time. We wanted to celebrate the end of the amazing heirloom season with an equally grand stage: in this case, frozen olive oil in the form of ice cream and "cheese" crisps. It may sound like a semi-dessert, but the character of the dish is purely savory.

TOMATOES
1½ pounds various large tomatoes (golden, heirloom, green zebra, etc.), the more colorful the better
3 tablespoons olive oil
1 teaspoon salt
Fresh black pepper

CRISPS
2 quarts pine nuts, soaked 1–2 hours
½ cup nutritional yeast
1 cup fresh lemon juice

2 teaspoons chipotle chile powder
2 teaspoons salt
1½ cups water
½ cup chopped fresh thyme

"ICE CREAM"
¾ quart olive oil, frozen
2 tablespoons raw agave
1½ teaspoons sea salt

TOMATOES Peel, halve, and seed tomatoes. Cut into small squares or rectangles. Season with olive oil, salt, and pepper.

CRISPS Pulse nuts in a food processor to break up. Add yeast, lemon juice, chile powder, salt, and water; blend until smooth. Add thyme; pulse until well combined. Spread on Teflex sheets to ⅛ inch thickness and dehydrate until crisp (1–2 days).

"ICE CREAM" Run olive oil in a Pacojet or a high-powered Vita-Mix with remaining ingredients.

ASSEMBLY Keep crisps warm in dehydrator. Divide tomatoes and arrange in various colors, spreading out on plates. Place 2 warm "cheese" crisps and 1 scoop olive oil "ice cream" on each plate. **SERVES 4**

lipstick sweet pepper and basil wrappers with marinated greens, truffle cream, and marcona almond paste

Dali inspired many chefs, including some of the most inventive in the world right now. Some are in Spain, including Ferran Adria of El Bulli. We chose his work as a basis for one of our recent dinners, and this dish—a combination of linear design with bold color and a surreal presence—was the result.

ALMOND PASTE
$3^1/2$ cups marcona almonds, soaked 8–10 hours
$1/2$ cup fresh lemon juice
$1/2$ cup water
1 cup olive oil
$1^1/2$ teaspoons salt
2 teaspoons nutritional yeast

SWEET PEPPER WRAPPERS
4 cups coconut meat
2 red bell peppers, chopped
$1/4$ cup beet juice
$1/2$ teaspoon sea salt

BASIL WRAPPERS
4 cups coconut meat
1 cup basil
$1/2$ teaspoon sea salt

GREENS
6 ounces baby greens (spinach, baby swiss chard, baby bok choy)
3 tablespoons olive oil
$1/2$ teaspoon salt
2 tablespoons fresh lemon juice
$1/4$ teaspoon black pepper

CREAM
1 cup cashews, soaked 1–2 hours
$3/4$ cup water
1 tablespoon truffle oil
2 tablespoons raw agave
$1/2$ teaspoon salt

ALMOND PASTE Process all ingredients in a food processor 3–5 minutes until smooth. Pour into quart containers. Set aside.

SWEET PEPPER WRAPPERS Blend all ingredients in a Vita-Mix until completely smooth. Spread in a thin layer over dehydrator Teflex sheets. Dehydrate 4–5 hours.

BASIL WRAPPERS Blend all ingredients in Vita-Mix until completely smooth. Spread in a thin layer over dehydrator Teflex sheets. Dehydrate 4–5 hours, then cut into thin strips and fold over accordion-folded cardstock paper. Dehydrate overnight.

GREENS Combine all ingredients and marinate at least 1 hour.

CREAM Blend all ingredients in a Vita-Mix until smooth.

ASSEMBLY Lay the sweet pepper wrappers flat on plates. Spread with a thin layer of truffle cream, followed by marinated greens. Drop pieces of almond paste on top of greens and cover with basil wrappers. **SERVES 4**

Of course, there will always be those who look only at technique, who ask "how," while others of a more curious nature ask "why." Personally, I have always preferred inspiration to information.

—Man Ray

inspiration

If food were simply about nourishment, life would be far less exciting. Instead, we are blessed with magical ingredients and recipes that offer us everything from a sense of euphoria to improved sleep to increased sex drive. I like to call these characteristics "inspirational" in honor of their ability to add to our life experiences in one way or another. Whether it is for a special symbolic occasion or simply everyday living, food contributes to the quality of our lives in both subtle and more potent ways.

History helps us here: generations pass down remedies, cures, and unique perspectives on certain foods. Tradition offers much in the way of putting reason behind certain preparations, and our own sensitivity, perhaps most importantly, directs our own choices. I know, for example, that raw cacao gives me energy, enlivens my palate, and creates positive thinking when I really need a boost. I'm quite confident that a cold, ripe red grapefruit will give me a buzz in the morning and that sweet peas in summer will always bring back memories.

This is also the age of superfoods—in part due to our society's hunger for a quick fix, but also because there are many more talented global foragers introducing products to the marketplace than ever before and more consumers taking notice of the wonders of certain foods. In the raw world, people are especially diligent in their perseverance and ability to communicate the benefits of these foods to the larger public. The results are more products available on the market and more creative people finding ways to use them.

Regardless of the cause of our inspiration, the ability of great food to enrich our lives through health, memory, or any positive form of stimulation remains one of life's great rewards.

white corn tamale, serrano-spiced portobello, raw cacao mole, and guacamole

Occasionally, the unusual taste of cacao fits perfectly with a savory dish—and this mole is an example of that. Rather than an unnecessary sweetness, it is nutty, deep, earthy, and, of course, very, very spicy. A few bites will wake up any palate in no time.

TAMALE
5 cups white corn kernels, divided
2 medium tomatoes, seeded and minced
1 red bell pepper, seeded and minced
$^1/_4$ cup chopped sun-dried tomatoes
$1^1/_4$ cups pine nuts, soaked 1–2 hours
$1^1/_4$ cups cashews, soaked 1–2 hours
1 teaspoon sea salt
$^3/_4$ teaspoon nutritional yeast
2 tablespoons minced red onion
2 tablespoons chopped fresh cilantro
1 clove garlic, peeled and minced
$^3/_4$ cup fresh lime juice

PORTOBELLO
4 portobello mushrooms, cut in half and into 8 slices
  per side
3 tablespoons olive oil
1 serrano chile, seeded and minced
Salt and freshly ground black pepper

MOLE
6 dried ancho/chipotle chiles, soaked 2–3 hours and
  drained
$^1/_2$ cup chopped red onion
2 cloves garlic, minced
2 tablespoons sunflower seeds, soaked 4–6 hours and
  drained

$^1/_2$ cup almond butter
$^1/_2$ cup raisins, soaked 20–30 minutes
6 tablespoons olive oil
1 cup water
2 tablespoons raw agave
2 teaspoons ground cumin
$^1/_2$ teaspoon ground coriander
1 teaspoon salt
$^1/_4$ teaspoon cayenne
1 cup cacao powder

CORNHUSKS
Soak 6 cornhusks in warm water for 1–2 hours

GUACAMOLE
3 ripe avocados, peeled, pitted, and roughly chopped
1 large handful cilantro leaves, finely chopped
2 tablespoons fresh lime juice
1 teaspoon sea salt
$^1/_2$ scallion, finely chopped
$^1/_2$ red chile, finely minced
1 jalapeño, seeded and minced

GARNISH
Cacao powder
Cilantro leaves

TAMALE Place $1^1/_2$ cups corn, the tomatoes, and the bell pepper in a bowl; set aside. In a food processor, blend the remaining ingredients until very smooth. Pour into bowl with other ingredients and mix well with hands.

PORTOBELLO Toss mushrooms with olive oil, serrano, salt, and pepper, then spread on Teflex sheets to dehydrate for 12–24 hours. Mix corn filling with portobello or reserve and serve on the side with tamales.

MOLE Blend all ingredients in a Vita-Mix until smooth.

CORNHUSKS Dry the cornhusks carefully. Lay cornhusks flat and place about $^1/_2$ cup corn mixture onto the center of each. Fold the bottom up over the filling and then fold the sides over. Using the husk strips, tie the tops of each tamale. Place the tamales in dehydrator for 2 hours.

GUACAMOLE Place all ingredients in a small bowl and mash well with a fork.

ASSEMBLY Spoon a generous amount of mole sauce on each plate, and set 2 tamales on sauce. Spoon Guacamole on top and garnish with cacao powder and cilantro leaves. SERVES 4–6

bitter broccoli ravioli and pine nut "cheese" in chocolate wrappers with orange powder and pinot noir sauce

One of the main dishes from a cacao dinner I hosted, this dish features ravioli where the "pasta" are made from cacao—it is one of the most straightforward preparations I have offered but so powerful and to the point that less is more. It has all of the elements—bitter, salty, sour, and sweet—that combine to create a complex harmony of flavor.

"CHEESE"
1 cup pine nuts, soaked 1–2 hours
2 tablespoons fresh lemon juice
$1/4$ teaspoon salt
$1/2$ teaspoon nutritional yeast
$1/2$ scallion

RABE
2 cups roughly chopped broccoli rabe
Juice of 1 lemon
3 tablespoons olive oil
$1/4$ teaspoon salt
$1/4$ teaspoon black pepper

WRAPPERS
2 cups young coconut meat
4 tablespoons raw cacao powder
$1/4$ teaspoon salt

SAUCE
2 cups Pinot Noir
$1/2$ cup pomegranate juice
1 tablespoon black peppercorns
1 small sprig rosemary
$1/4$ cup dried cherries
Juice of 1 lemon

POWDER
1 cup orange zest

"CHEESE" Process all ingredients in a food processor until smooth.

RABE Toss all ingredients in a large bowl. Spread on Teflex sheets and dehydrate 30 minutes.

WRAPPERS Blend all ingredients in a Vita-Mix until very smooth. Spread mixture in a thin even layer over a Teflex sheet and dehydrate 3 hours. Store in plastic wrap in refrigerator until ready to use. Remove from refrigerator and allow the mixture to adjust to room temperature prior to use. Trim edges and cut into 16 squares.

SAUCE In a shallow pan, dehydrate Pinot Noir, pomegranate juice, black peppercorns, and rosemary until liquid has reduced by 50 percent, about 8 hours. Strain liquid and blend with remaining ingredients.

POWDER Spread zest on Teflex sheets and cover with a dehydrator screen. Dehydrate overnight until completely dry. Blend in Vita-Mix into a powder.

ASSEMBLY Mix broccoli rabe into "cheese" for the filling. To prepare the ravioli, place a teaspoon of filling just off center on each square and fold over, pressing each together softly. Line the raviolis in a row on plates and drizzle with sauce; garnish with orange powder. **SERVES 4**

chocolate chili tacos with marinated arugula, pear tomatoes, and pignoli "sour cream"

Cacao, the raw cocoa bean—not to be confused with processed or sweetened chocolate—is quickly becoming the most well-known superfood in the raw world. It is an excellent source of magnesium and ananamide, which is known as the "bliss chemical," bringing on a sense of well-being. It is a stimulant and, although slightly pungent, its unique taste is pleasant, especially in a recipe like this.

TACO SHELLS

3 cups fresh corn
1 1/2 cups chopped red bell pepper
3/4 cup flax meal
1/2 cup water
1 tablespoon fresh lime juice
1 1/2 teaspoons chili powder
1 1/2 teaspoons sea salt
2 teaspoons cumin
2 tablespoons raw cocoa powder

"SOUR CREAM"

2 cups pine nuts, soaked 1–2 hours
1 cup water
1/2 cup olive oil
3 tablespoons fresh lemon juice
1 teaspoon sea salt

ARUGULA

1 quart fresh arugula, packed and gently torn
Olive oil
Sea salt
Black pepper

TOMATOES

1 pint pear tomatoes, halved
3 tablespoons olive oil
1/2 teaspoon salt
Black pepper
1/4 cup julienned basil

GARNISH

1 avocado, optional
10 basil leaves, coarsely chopped, optional

TACO SHELLS Blend all ingredients in a Vita-Mix until smooth. Spread on Teflex sheets to 1/4-inch thickness in 5- or 6-inch rounds; dehydrate at 118 degrees F for 3–4 hours; flip and dehydrate 30 minutes more. Fold in half to shape into taco shells; dehydrate overnight.

"SOUR CREAM" Blend all ingredients in Vita-Mix until completely smooth. Pour into quart containers.

ARUGULA Toss arugula with enough olive oil to lightly coat, then add sea salt and black pepper to taste. Place arugula in a bowl and cover with plastic wrap; let sit in a dehydrator at 118 degrees F for 15–20 minutes, until wilted.

TOMATOES Toss tomatoes with olive oil, salt, and pepper; dehydrate 3 hours. Add basil.

ASSEMBLY Divide the arugula among the taco shells; add pear tomatoes and a generous amount of "sour cream." Top with avocado and fresh basil. SERVES 4–6

cinnamon graham cookie
with marshmallow crème and
dark chocolate fondue

Admittedly, this is a raw version of s'mores—I had been talking about making this dish for many weeks when I needed a chocolate dessert for a contemporary menu we had been planning. It is comfort food in disguise and a potent version at that.

COOKIE
5 cups cashew flour
2 1/2 cups oat flour
3/4 cup water
1 3/4 cups maple syrup
2 tablespoons vanilla extract
1 tablespoon sea salt
2 tablespoons cinnamon

CRÈME
2 cups cashews, soaked 1–2 hours
1 cup coconut meat
1 tablespoon vanilla extract
1/2 teaspoon salt

1/2 cup raw agave
1/4 cup coconut oil
1 small (1.25-ounce) bottle Lorann Marshmallow Concentrated Oil

FONDUE
4 cups maple syrup
2 1/2 cups raw cocoa powder
2 cups coconut oil
1 teaspoon vanilla extract
1/2 teaspoon salt

GARNISH
2 tablespoons cinnamon

COOKIE Mix ingredients in a medium-size bowl by hand. Spread flat to 1/8 inch thick on dehydrator screens. Dehydrate at 115 degrees F for 4 hours. Make an incision with the back of a knife for six rectangles. Dehydrate another 6 hours, then separate pieces. Keep well sealed, at room temperature, until ready to serve.

CRÈME Blend all ingredients in a Vita-Mix until smooth. Pour into a plastic-lined half sheet pan; refrigerate overnight or freeze 1–2 hours prior to serving.

FONDUE Whisk all ingredients in a large bowl. Blend in batches in Vita-Mix. Pour into half sheet pan and store in freezer.

ASSEMBLY Bring crème to room temperature at least 20 minutes prior to serving. Warm chocolate and cookies slightly in dehydrator. Place 1 cookie on a plate. Carefully spread a generous amount of crème on top and pour an even more generous amount of fondue over that, allowing it to slightly run off onto the plate. Set another cookie on top, but off center, exposing the crème and fondue. Sprinkle the plate with cinnamon. SERVES 4

raspberry sundae with vanilla bean "ice cream," chocolate anise syrup, and candied walnuts

This is a more straightforward dessert, a sundae that can include any number of berries. I love raspberries, but blueberry and anise work equally well together, as do strawberries or cherries. It's pleasant enough to simply eat a big spoonful of berries with the chocolate sauce poured over them!

RASPBERRIES
1/4 cup raw agave
2 cups raspberries, divided

WALNUTS
2 cups walnuts, soaked overnight, drained, and
   dehydrated 24 hours
1/4 cup maple powder
1/4 cup maple syrup
1 teaspoon vanilla extract
Pinch salt
1/2 tablespoon cinnamon

SYRUP
1/2 cup plus 2 tablespoons raw agave
1/2 cup melted coconut oil

1/2 teaspoon vanilla extract
1/4 teaspoon sea salt
1 cup plus 2 tablespoons cocoa powder
3/4 teaspoon hazelnut extract

"ICE CREAM"
1 1/2 cups cashews, soaked 1–2 hours
1/2 cup coconut meat
1/2 vanilla bean, scraped
1/4 teaspoon sea salt
1/4 cup raw agave
1/4 cup plus 2 tablespoons coconut oil

GARNISH
1/4 cup cacao nibs
Mint sprigs

RASPBERRIES Blend agave and 1 cup raspberries in a Vita-Mix. Stir in remaining raspberries.

WALNUTS Mix nuts well with all ingredients and dehydrate 48 hours.

SYRUP Blend all ingredients in Vita-Mix until smooth.

"ICE CREAM" Blend all ingredients until smooth in Vita-Mix. Process in an ice cream maker and freeze.

ASSEMBLY Layer the raspberries, ice cream, and syrup. Top with walnuts, nibs, and mint sprigs. SERVES 6

saffron avgolemono, portobello "meatballs," oregano cream, and lemon balm

Raw food is beginning to develop its own culinary language, but at present, many dishes are still relying on descriptions based on traditional, often non-vegetarian recipes. This is not an absolute necessity, but it does make the food more interesting to a newcomer, who can perhaps identify with it a bit more. *Avgolemono* means "egg-lemon" in Greek. It gets its texture from the egg cooking and thickening. Of course, in our raw version, that is unnecessary—interestingly, the velvety texture is quite close here.

AVGOLEMONO
1/2 cup chopped jicama
1/4 cup cashews, soaked 3–4 hours
3 tablespoons lemon juice
1 teaspoon lemon zest
3 tablespoons olive oil
1/2 teaspoon salt
1 teaspoon saffron, dissolved in 3 cups warm water
Black pepper to taste

"MEATBALLS"
2 portobello mushroom caps
1/4 cup walnuts
1/4 cup tahini

2 tablespoons olive oil
1/2 cup chopped zucchini
2 tablespoons chopped parsley
Salt and pepper to taste

CREAM
2 cups cashews, soaked 1–2 hours
1/2 cup water
2 tablespoons raw agave
1 teaspoon salt
1/2 cup fresh oregano

GARNISH
Fresh saffron
1 tablespoon fresh lemon balm

AVGOLEMONO Blend all ingredients in a Vita-Mix until smooth. Warm in dehydrator for 3–4 hours.

"MEATBALLS" In a food processor, process ingredients until well combined but not fully puréed. Form into small "meatballs" and dehydrate 5 hours.

CREAM Blend all ingredients in Vita-Mix until smooth. Chill in the refrigerator until firm.

ASSEMBLY Warm avgolemono in a baking pan in dehydrator—place "meatballs" in each soup dish, and top with a couple of threads of saffron and lemon balm; drizzle with oregano cream. SERVES 4–6

cacao crêpes and sweet mint custard with black cacao sauce

When I was first experimenting with raw cacao, it was challenging to use—it was not yet available in powder form, and the taste was unusual, so I was a bit unsure of it—but the dried beans actually reacted well to certain recipes, especially those where a soft texture is needed. This dish is pure classic in flavor.

CRÊPES
1 quart flax meal
1 quart apples, peeled, cored, and chopped
2 cups chopped coconut meat
2 cups cocoa powder
1/4 cup fresh lemon juice
2 quarts water
2 tablespoons maple syrup
1/4 cup raw agave
2 1/4 teaspoons salt

MINT CUSTARD
2 cups cashews, soaked 4–6 hours
1 cup coconut meat
1 tablespoon vanilla extract
1/2 teaspoon salt
1/2 cup raw agave
1/4 cup coconut oil
3/4 teaspoon peppermint oil

JAM
1 pint raspberries
1/4 cup Irish moss

1/4 cup raw agave
1 tablespoon lemon zest

SAUCE
2 1/2 cups raw agave
1 cup cocoa powder
1/4 cup carob powder
1/2 teaspoon vanilla
1/4 teaspoon salt
1/4 cup maple syrup
1 1/4 cups coconut oil

BANANA "ICE CREAM"
1 cup cashews, soaked 1–2 hours
1/2 cup coconut meat
1/2 cup raw agave
1 1/4 cups water
2 fresh bananas, peeled
1 teaspoon lemon juice
1/4 vanilla bean, scraped
Pinch sea salt
1/2 cup coconut oil

CRÊPES Blend all ingredients in a Vita-Mix. Spread thinly into 4- or 5-inch rounds on dehydrator Teflex sheets (9 per tray). Dehydrate 5–6 hours, or until dry but very pliable.

MINT CUSTARD Blend ingredients in Vita-Mix until smooth. Place in quart containers and freeze. Run in a Pacojet, freeze, and then run again. Makes 1 quart.

JAM Blend all ingredients in a food processor, chill for 3 hours.

SAUCE Blend ingredients in Vita-Mix until smooth.

BANANA "ICE CREAM" Blend all ingredients in Vita-Mix until very smooth. Pour into an ice cream maker and follow manufacturer's instructions.

ASSEMBLY Fill the crêpes with mint custard and jam. Scoop banana "ice cream" to the side and pour chocolate sauce over top. **SERVES 4–6**

frozen mint panna cotta with marshmallow whip, vanilla wafers, and bittersweet cacao sauce

This requires marshmallow extract, but if it is unavailable, extra vanilla bean will be fine. As with many desserts, the components of this will work well with any number of recipes.

PANNA COTTA
3 cups cashews, soaked 1–2 hours
$1/2$ cup coconut meat
$1^1/2$ cups raw agave
2 cups water
4 teaspoons vanilla extract
$1^1/2$ teaspoons nonalcoholic peppermint extract
$1/4$ teaspoon sea salt
1 cup coconut oil
6 tablespoons spinach juice
$2/3$ cup chopped pistachios
$1/2$ cup cacao nibs

WHIP
$1^1/2$ cups cashews, soaked 1–2 hours
$1^1/2$ cups coconut meat
1 cup raw agave nectar
$3/4$ cup extra-virgin coconut oil
$1/4$ cup water
2 teaspoons vanilla extract
$1/2$ teaspoon sea salt
1–2 bottles marshmallow extract

WAFERS
3 cups fine cashew flour
$1^3/4$ cups almond flour
$1/4$ cup coconut oil
1 cup maple syrup
4 teaspoons vanilla extract
4 vanilla beans, scraped
$1^1/2$ teaspoons sea salt
Lemon juice
1/2 teaspoon cinnamon

SAUCE
3 cups raw agave
$1^1/2$ cups raw cacao powder
$1/4$ cup raw carob powder
$1/2$ teaspoon vanilla extract
$1/4$ teaspoon sea salt
$1/2$ cup coconut oil

PANNA COTTA Blend all ingredients except pistachios and cacao in a Vita-Mix until smooth. Stir in pistachios and nibs. Freeze in custard molds until ready to use.

WHIP Blend all ingredients in Vita-Mix until very smooth. Chill in freezer 3–4 hours, then whip in a blender.

WAFERS Mix ingredients in a medium-size bowl by hand. Spread to $1/8$ inch thick on Teflex sheets and dehydrate 4–5 hours. Cut into desired shapes and place on dehydrator screens; dehydrate an additional 4–5 hours.

SAUCE Blend ingredients in Vita-Mix until smooth.

ASSEMBLY Unmold panna cotta onto plates—garnish with whip and drizzle sauce over the top. Stick two wafers into each panna cotta. SERVES 4–6

chocolate cake with sweet cherries, spiced cinnamon "ice cream," and cayenne-cacao syrup

Everyone has a favorite chocolate cake recipe, which makes it a challenge to come up with a new one. This unusual recipe is made with cashew flour, which gives it a dense, almost flourless character as well as a nuttier base than a typical cake with eggs, sugar, and white flour.

CAKE
4 1/2 cups fine cashew flour (passed through a tamis or fine sifter)
3 cups cocoa powder
3/4 cup maple syrup
3/4 cup raw agave
1 1/2 cups water
1/2 tablespoon sea salt
3/4 teaspoon vanilla extract
1/2 teaspoon cinnamon

CHERRIES
2 cups cherries
1/4 cup raw agave
Pinch cayenne and salt

"ICE CREAM"
1 1/2 cups young coconut meat
1 cup cashews, soaked 4 hours
1/4 cup raw agave
1 tablespoon cinnamon
1/4 teaspoon cayenne
1/2 teaspoon ancho chile powder

SYRUP
3 cups raw agave
1 cup raw cacao powder
1/4 cup raw carob powder
1/2 teaspoon vanilla extract
1/2–1 teaspoon cayenne
1/4 teaspoon sea salt
1/2 cup coconut oil

CAKE Mix together cashew flour and cocoa powder in a large bowl. Add remaining ingredients; mix well with hands. Line 2 half sheet pans with parchment. Evenly distribute batter into 2 pans; press into pans in an even layer. Dehydrate in bottom of dehydrators overnight. Flip onto cutting board and trim edges. Place on screens. Dehydrate another 4–6 hours, cool, and then cut cake into shapes as desired using a cookie cutter, ring mold, or knife.

CHERRIES Combine all ingredients and dehydrate 4 hours.

"ICE CREAM" Process all ingredients in a Vita-Mix and freeze in an ice cream maker according to manufacturer's instructions.

SYRUP Blend all ingredients in Vita-Mix until smooth.

ASSEMBLY Pour syrup on each plate; set cake on syrup and top each serving with cherries and ice cream.
SERVES 8

oreo cookie with cream filling, vanilla bean "ice cream," and black cocoa syrup

This is chocolate and vanilla, simply presented in a new form. I swore off my youthful penchant for junk food many years ago, but Kristen, a very talented chef I worked with, tempts me with these recipes and I feel that I am regressing.

COOKIE
4 cups raw cocoa powder
4 cups oat flour
$1^1/2$ teaspoons Himalayan salt
1 cup maple syrup
1 cup raw agave
3 tablespoons coconut oil, melted
$1^1/2$ teaspoons vanilla extract

CREAM FILLING
3 cups cashews, soaked
1 cup coconut meat
1 tablespoon vanilla extract
$1/2$ teaspoon salt
$1/2$ cup raw agave
$3/4$ cup coconut oil

"ICE CREAM" (SEE PAGE 96)

SYRUP
$2^1/2$ cups raw agave
1 cup cocoa powder
$1/4$ cup carob powder
$1/2$ teaspoon vanilla
$1/4$ teaspoon salt
$1/4$ cup maple syrup
$1^1/4$ cups coconut oil

GARNISH
Fresh black peppermint

COOKIE Mix together dry ingredients in a large bowl. Add remaining ingredients to dry ingredients. Mix well with hands. Line a 9 x 13-inch pan with parchment paper. Press into pan in an even layer and dehydrate overnight. Flip onto a cutting board, cut into circles with a ring mold or cookie cutter, and place on dehydrator screens and dehydrate another 4–6 hours.

CREAM FILLING Blend all ingredients until smooth in a Vita-Mix. Pour into a plastic-lined half sheet pan; refrigerate overnight or freeze 1–2 hours prior to serving.

SYRUP Blend all ingredients in Vita-Mix until smooth.

ASSEMBLY Fill cookies with cream filling (like Oreos). Serve with chocolate sauce and "ice cream," and garnish with peppermint. SERVES 10–12

susie q, raspberry sauce, and red curry "ice cream"

Whenever I had a little extra money from mowing lawns or delivering newspapers as a child, I would buy myself a Susie Q— in hindsight, I can't imagine how I could eat all that sugar and white flour without crashing in about ten minutes. I can't guess how many times I have challenged my sous chefs with a nearly impossible-to-create raw food dish, but they did it again with this.

CAKE
9 cups fine cashew flour (passed through a tami)
5 cups cocoa powder
3/4 tablespoon sea salt
2 1/4 cups raw agave
3 cups water
1 1/2 teaspoons vanilla extract
3/4 teaspoon cinnamon

CREAM
6 cups cashews, soaked 1–2 hours
4 cups coconut meat
2 1/2 cups water
2 1/2 cups raw agave
2 cups melted coconut oil
2 vanilla beans, scraped
1 teaspoon sea salt

SAUCE
2 cups raspberries
1/2 teaspoon vanilla
1/2 cup raw agave

"ICE CREAM"
1 cup cashews, soaked 1–2 hours
4 ounces coconut meat
1/2 cup raw agave
1 1/2 cups water
2 teaspoons vanilla extract
2 1/2 teaspoons red curry powder
Pinch sea salt
1/2 cup coconut oil

CAKE Mix together dry ingredients in a large bowl. Add remaining ingredients; mix well with hands. Line 2 half sheet pans with parchment. Gently press into 2 pans; smooth into 1-inch even layers. Dehydrate in bottom of dehydrators 6–8 hours. Flip onto a cutting board and trim edges. Place on screens. Dehydrate another 6 hours.

CREAM Blend ingredients in a Vita-Mix until very smooth; freeze. Run in a Pacojet; freeze.

SAUCE Blend all ingredients in Vita-Mix until smooth.

"ICE CREAM" Blend all ingredients in Vita-Mix until very smooth. Pour into an ice cream maker and follow manufacturer's instructions.

ASSEMBLY Cut cake into 2 x 4-inch rectangles. Make "sandwiches" by spreading 1/4 cup vanilla cream between two cake rectangles. Serve with ice cream and raspberry sauce on the side. SERVES 4–6

yellow squash pasta, creamy saffron broth, and wild fennel

As a young kitchen apprentice at the Sicilian restaurant Malvasia, I remember the chef receiving his weekly delivery of sardines from Italy and preparing the classic Pasta con Sarde with Wild Fennel and Golden Raisins. The aroma of the fennel and saffron cooking together was so magical and the sweet spiciness so captivating that his kitchen transported you to a Mediterranean island at that moment.

PASTA
3 cups yellow squash, peeled and cut to fit a spiral slicer
1 head fennel, shaved and tossed in olive oil, salt, and black pepper, then dehydrated 3–4 hours
1 cup Pine Nut "Parmesan" (see page 38)
1 cup sliced cherry tomatoes, dehydrated overnight
1/4 cup pitted and chopped green olives
1/4 cup pine nuts
1/4 cup white raisins, soaked 2 hours in 1/4 cup white wine and 1 teaspoon lemon juice

BROTH
2 cups water
3 tablespoons saffron
1/2 cup cashews, soaked 1–2 hours
Salt
2 tablespoons olive oil
Salt and black pepper to taste

2 tablespoons lemon juice
2 tablespoons raw agave

BREAD CRUMBS
1 cup flax meal
1/4 cup dried basil
1 tablespoon dried oregano
2 yellow squash, rough chopped
1/2 cup walnuts, soaked 8–10 hours
1 teaspoon sea salt
1/2 teaspoon black pepper
3 tablespoons olive oil
1/2 shallot, minced
1 tablespoon nutritional yeast
1 tablespoon raw agave
1 tablespoon fresh lemon juice

GARNISH
Fennel fronds
Pine Nut "Parmesan"

PASTA Mix all ingredients together in a large bowl.

BROTH Combine water with saffron and place in a dehydrator for 2 hours to infuse. Add to remaining ingredients and blend until smooth.

BREAD CRUMBS Place flax meal, basil, and oregano in a medium-size bowl; set aside. Process remaining ingredients in a food processor until smooth. Add to bowl with flax meal and stir until well combined. Spread on Teflex sheets.

Dehydrate at 115 degrees F for 24–36 hours until almost completely dry but still a bit pliable. Crumble onto screens and dehydrate until crisp.

ASSEMBLY Toss pasta with 1/2 of the broth and 2/3 of the bread crumbs. Pour the remaining broth into shallow bowls, add pasta, and garnish with generous amounts of "Parmesan," fennel fronds, and remaining bread crumbs.
SERVES 4–6

oyster mushrooms and hijiki caviar with leek and brazil nut truffle foam

This could very well be a New Year's appetizer, with its decadent creamy truffle sauce. Most interesting is the "shell," which makes these very easy to present and eat. It would work equally well as an hors d'oeuvre.

MUSHROOMS
2 cups water
Juice of 2 lemons
1 tablespoon lemon zest
1 cup cashews, soaked 4–6 hours
2 tablespoons raw agave
Salt and pepper
20 oyster mushrooms

SHELLS
1 recipe black and white dumpling wrappers (see page 60)

CAVIAR
1 cup hijiki seaweed, soaked 1 hour and drained
3 tablespoons sesame oil

1 tablespoon raw agave
1 tablespoon nama shoyu

FOAM
1 cup chopped leek
$1/4$ cup white truffle oil, divided
$2^1/2$ tablespoons salt, divided
4 cups Brazil nuts, soaked 8–10 hours
8 cups water
1 teaspoon nutritional yeast
1 cup chard, stemmed

GARNISH
1 bunch chives, chopped

MUSHROOMS Blend all ingredients except mushrooms in a Vita-Mix. Cut mushrooms into oyster shape by trimming edges a bit and toss with the lemon cream. Place in a dehydrator to warm for 1 hour.

SHELLS Cut each sheet into 16 squares, trim edges to form rounds, then mold in bottom of 4-ounce soufflé containers; dehydrate another 3–4 hours.

CAVIAR Chop hijiki into very small caviar-size pieces. Toss with remaining ingredients.

FOAM Toss leek with 1 tablespoon truffle oil and $1/2$ table-spoon salt; spread onto a half sheet pan and dehydrate at 118 degrees F for 6 hours. Blend Brazil nuts and water until smooth; strain through a fine chinois. Place Brazil nut milk back in Vita-Mix and add remaining ingredients, including marinated leek, and blend until smooth.

ASSEMBLY Place a teaspoon of foam in each "shell" and top with an oyster mushroom. Drizzle with more sauce and top with caviar and chives. SERVES 4–6

"...we get to think of life as an inexhaustible well. Yet everything happens only a certain number of times, and a very small number, really....How many more times will you watch the full moon rise? Perhaps twenty. And yet it all seems limitless."

—Paul Bowles

spice

The best expression, whether through food, literature, art, or film, often takes us on a journey to a place either new or forgotten. Transporting is the word often referenced when a meal not only excites our senses but also removes us from the present and places us into the captivating and unknown. I know of no other cuisine that is more sensual and deeply rooted in history and mystery as that which makes ample use of spices. There are many factors that contribute to this.

Spices have been an important economic commodity throughout history and have had a major impact on exploration, trade, and travel. They are beloved by many nations for the exotic flavors they lend to cooking, as well as for their many therapeutic and medicinal properties. I was first captivated by spices during an extended trip to Morocco, where the outdoor markets offered enormous baskets of them—filled with the deepest hues of oranges, reds, yellows, and ochres—like a glowing sunset.

Over the years, I have been introduced to dishes from around the world—most of my favorites have a powerful yet refined use of spices, from coriander to saffron to my favorite, white cardamom. These flavors and colors not only have influenced my cooking and palate but also have given me "taste memories" that will stay with me forever. I am remembering the first vegetable tagine I had in Fez so many years ago—it is as distinct as if I first tried it this morning and yet is so far away.

Spices must be used in moderation and respected for their inherent character. They must always be fresh and well stored, preferably whole or recently ground. Utilize them as you might a photo album or a brief vacation—let them transport you to another land and place far away, or let them bring you home again.

black sesame paratha, spiced cucumbers, and mango–green papaya chutney

Indian dishes are excellent for use in raw food preparation because of their ability to utilize ingredients—cucumbers and fruits, for example—that work so well in their raw state. It is also relatively easy to dress up an Indian dish with a simple chutney or spice mix in a way that it becomes something far more interesting. This paratha is a very easy dish to put together once the crisp is prepared. It is a great snack or casual starter for a dinner party or luncheon.

PARATHA
1 cup flax meal
3/4 cup walnuts, soaked 1–2 hours
3/4 cup cashews, soaked 2 hours
2 yellow squash, chopped
1/2 teaspoon salt
1/4 teaspoon black pepper
1/4 cup olive oil
1 tablespoon nutritional yeast
1/2 teaspoon cumin
1/4 cup black sesame seeds

CUCUMBERS
1 large cucumber, peeled, halved lengthwise,
  and seeded
1/4 teaspoon cayenne pepper
1/4 teaspoon cumin
1 tablespoon fresh lime juice
Sea salt to taste

CHUTNEY
2 ripe mangoes, cut into small dice
2 tablespoons raw agave
1/4 teaspoon sesame oil
1 medium green papaya, shredded
1 teaspoon minced green chili
1 tablespoon cracked coriander seed
Sea salt
1/4 cup cilantro

GARNISH
2 avocados, diced
1 teaspoon paprika plus 1 tablespoon for garnish
2 tablespoons fresh lime juice
Salt
Cilantro leaves

PARATHA Place flax meal in a medium-size bowl; set aside. Blend remaining ingredients in a Vita-Mix until smooth. Add to flax meal and combine well. Spread 3-inch circles, 1/4 inch thick, on Teflex sheets and dehydrate 8–10 hours.

CUCUMBERS Cut the cucumbers into 1/8-inch-thick half moons and combine with remaining ingredients. Allow to marinate at least 1 hour.

CHUTNEY In a food processor, combine 1/3 of the mango, the agave, and the sesame oil. In a large bowl, combine with remaining mango and ingredients except cilantro; dehydrate 3 hours. Let cool and stir in cilantro.

ASSEMBLY On individual plates or a serving tray, lay paratha flat, top with avocado, cucumbers, and then chutney. Garnish with paprika and cilantro leaves. SERVES 4–6

citrus tart, raspberry leaf–infused cherry sauce, and rosewater "ice cream"

I try to stay away from using the word "sexy" to describe food that I work with, mainly because it is now overused and I have been given plenty of teasing for my own overindulgence of it as a descriptor. Yet, it is the best way for me to explain this dish—sexy.

SAUCE
1 cup fresh cherries, or thawed if frozen
3 tablespoons raw agave
1/4 teaspoon raspberry leaf extract
Water

CRUST
1 1/2 cups shredded coconut
1 1/4 cup cashew flour
1/4 teaspoon salt
1/4 cup raw agave
1/4 cup coconut oil

FILLING
1 1/2 cups cashews, soaked at least 1 hour
1/4 cup plus 2 tablespoons fresh lemon juice
1/4 cup plus 2 tablespoons raw agave
1/4 cup plus 2 tablespoons coconut oil, melted

1/4 cup water
1/2 teaspoon vanilla extract
1 1/2 tablespoons lime zest
2 tablespoons finely minced orange zest
1/4 teaspoon sea salt
1/4 vanilla bean, scraped

"ICE CREAM"
1/2 cup cashews, soaked 1–2 hours
1 cup macadamia nuts, soaked 1–2 hours
1/4 cup coconut meat
3/4 cup raw agave
1 cup water
2 teaspoons vanilla extract
1 tablespoon rosewater extract
Pinch sea salt
1/2 cup coconut oil

SAUCE Blend cherries, agave, and extract; add just enough water to thin to sauce consistency.

CRUST Mix all ingredients together well by hand. Press into a plastic-lined 9-inch tart pan to desired thickness. Optional: dehydrate 24–48 hours. Chill crust in freezer for at least 15 minutes or until ready to fill.

FILLING Blend all ingredients in a Vita-Mix until very smooth. Fill crusts and chill in freezer overnight. Remove pies from metal tart shells. Store in freezer.

"ICE CREAM" Blend all ingredients in Vita-Mix until smooth. Pour into an ice cream maker and follow manufacturer's instructions.

ASSEMBLY Pour a small pool of sauce on a plate—top with a slice of tart and place ice cream to one side.
SERVES 4–6

heirloom tomato pavé and preserved lemon dressing with green olives and pine nuts

I'll never forget the day I returned from a two-week trip to Morocco, filled with ideas and taste memories. I could not wait to get into the kitchen at my original restaurant, Matthew's, to experiment with what I had learned and with some of the ingredient combinations that I had been thinking about. It was this first Moroccan trip where I found my footing as a chef and began to learn how to "reinterpret" food in a way that it would remain grounded and focused but also take on its own originality. In Morocco, I had tasted an amazing lemon chicken with olives, preserved lemon, pine nuts, and saffron. My version of "lemon chicken" remained on my menu for many years, and though I haven't had chicken or poultry in years, the memory is of the nutty, sweet-and-sour lemon flavor. I try to incorporate it into food whenever I can. This dish was a big success at my restaurant The Plant and is relatively easy to make as long as you have good, ripe, firm tomatoes.

PAVÉ
4 large golden, green, or red tomatoes, peeled and cored

DRESSING
1/4 cup preserved lemons
2 tablespoons fresh lemon juice
1/4 cup almond oil
2 tablespoons raw agave nectar

3 tablespoons pitted green olives
Salt
Pepper
Water

GARNISH
Pine nuts
1/4 cup julienned preserved lemon peel
Cilantro leaves

PAVÉ Slice tomatoes thinly lengthwise by running a sharp knife parallel to flat surface. Trim into squares.

DRESSING Process all ingredients in a food processor. Add water to thin if necessary.

ASSEMBLY Brush a small amount of dressing on tomato slices to coat lightly. Overlap them in a long row or a large square. Drizzle with more sauce, sprinkle with pine nuts and preserved lemon slices, and garnish with cilantro leaves. SERVES 4

shiitake bisteeya with ginger-cilantro sauce, candied almonds, and wilted spinach

I credit my ability to be creative with raw food to the exotic foods I experimented with over many years as a traditional chef and as a consumer of pretty much any food that was available throughout the world. The first time I saw a bisteeya, it was awe-inspiring. Standing in the courtyard of a private palace in Morocco, I saw the chefs carrying silver trays with the giant crackling, sugar-coated, savory pies known as bisteeya. These were filled with chicken, pigeon, almonds, sugar, egg, and spices—and were utterly delicious. In fact, on a food tour of Morocco, I visited a cooking school outside of Rabat, which specialized in teaching the preparation of Warka, the pastry specifically made for this dish. The school was mesmerizing—for its silence and also for the fact that it was only available to women.

To serve Bisteeya implies a celebration of sorts, and that is what we had in mind for our Moroccan Friday at The Plant with this raw version. I can't claim that it is as crispy as the original version, but it is quite tasty, nonetheless.

BISTEEYA WRAPPERS
Recipe coconut wrappers (see page 221)

BISTEEYA MUSHROOMS
1 cup thinly sliced shiitake mushrooms
2 tablespoons olive oil
Salt
Black pepper

CANDIED ALMONDS
6 cups almonds
$1/3$ cup plus 1 tablespoon maple syrup
1 teaspoon vanilla extract
$1/2$ tablespoon sea salt
$1^1/2$ tablespoons ground cinnamon
$1^1/2$ cups maple powder

SAUCE
$1/4$ cup minced ginger
$1/4$ cup almonds, soaked 4 hours

1 cup water
2 tablespoons raw agave
$1/4$ cup cilantro leaves
Salt

SPINACH
1 cup young spinach leaves
1 tablespoon olive oil
1 teaspoon fresh lemon juice
$1/2$ teaspoon lemon zest
Salt and pepper

GARNISH
$1/4$ cup cilantro leaves
1 teaspoon cinnamon
1 teaspoon turmeric

BISTEEYA MUSHROOMS Toss shiitake slices with olive oil, salt, and pepper, then dehydrate on Teflex sheets for 30–60 minutes.

CANDIED ALMONDS Soak nuts overnight; drain. Dehydrate 24 hours. In a large bowl, coat dehydrated nuts with maple syrup. Combine vanilla, salt, cinnamon, and maple powder, and stir into nuts until they are well coated. Dehydrate on screens for 48 hours.

SAUCE Blend all ingredients in a Vita-Mix until smooth.

SPINACH Combine all ingredients and dehydrate 20 minutes.

ASSEMBLY Mix mushrooms with candied nuts, cilantro leaves, and enough sauce to bind them together.

Cut each sheet of wrappers into 3 strips, and cut those in half. Place a dollop of filling at the near end of wrapper and fold over, corner to corner, to make triangle shapes.

Scatter spinach on plates, top with bisteeya, and garnish with cinnamon and turmeric. **SERVES 4**

spring vegetable tagine with couscous, harissa, and cumin flatbread

Despite working with the far-out flavors and techniques associated with raw food, I still have a great respect for tradition. This is especially the case with Moroccan food, which I fell in love with many times. As a result, I was somewhat skeptical about my chance of success in reinterpreting a couscous dish, but it did work. The flavors were deep and exotic, and overall the dish was lighter than I expected. There are many variations, but this one keeps in tune with history, using classical and common ingredients.

TAGINE

ASPARAGUS AND TOMATOES
1 bunch asparagus, cut on a bias in 1 1/2-inch lengths
1/4 cup olive oil
Salt and pepper
1 pint cherry or pear tomatoes (preferably yellow and red)

VEGETABLE STOCK
2 stalks celery
1 carrot
1 tomato, crushed
2 cups water
1 sprig thyme
3 black peppercorns

FAVA BEANS AND MUSHROOMS
1 cup peeled fava beans
Olive oil
Salt and pepper
1 cup oyster mushrooms
1 cup cremini mushrooms

COUSCOUS
2 large jicama, peeled and roughly chopped
2/3 cup pine nuts
2 tablespoons nutritional yeast
2 tablespoons olive oil
Salt and pepper

ASPARAGUS AND TOMATOES Cut and slice asparagus, then toss in olive oil, salt, and pepper. Spread asparagus in a half sheet pan and dehydrate 3–4 hours. Halve pear tomatoes and toss with olive oil, salt, and pepper. Spread prepped tomatoes on Teflex sheets for 30 minutes to marinate.

VEGETABLE STOCK Juice the celery and carrot. Blend remaining ingredients, add celery and carrot juice, and strain. Dehydrate 1 hour.

FAVA BEANS AND MUSHROOMS Toss fava beans with olive oil, salt, and pepper; spread in half sheet pan with 1 1/2 cups vegetable stock, then dehydrate for 4 hours.

Slice oyster and cremini mushrooms. Toss mushrooms with olive oil and salt, then spread on Teflex sheets to dehydrate 1 hour. Add remaining vegetables and stock as needed just to cover.

COUSCOUS Process jicama and pine nuts until very fine. Add remaining ingredients.

continued on page 122

HARISSA

4 fresh red chiles
Sea salt
1 teaspoon ground caraway seeds
1 tablespoon smoked paprika
1 heaped teaspoon ground cumin seeds
1 clove garlic
1 red pepper, cored, seeded, and roughly chopped
1 plum tomato
1 tablespoon red wine
1 tablespoon lemon juice
2 tablespoons olive oil
Salt

FLATBREAD

1 cup flax meal
1 tablespoon dried basil
1 tablespoon dried oregano
2 teaspoons cumin
2 yellow squash, roughly chopped
1 1/2 cups walnuts, soaked 6 hours
1 1/2 teaspoons salt
1/2 teaspoon cayenne pepper
1/4 cup olive oil
1 shallot, minced
1 tablespoon nutritional yeast
2 tablespoons raw agave
1 tablespoon sumac

HARISSA Blend all ingredients except salt in a Vita-Mix until very smooth. Season with salt as needed.

FLATBREAD Place flax meal, basil, and oregano in a medium-size bowl and set aside. Process remaining ingredients except sumac in a food processor until smooth. Add to bowl with flax meal and stir until well combined. Spread on Teflex sheets to 1/2-inch thickness; sprinkle with sumac. Dehydrate 6–8 hours until almost completely dry but still pliable. Transfer bread to dehydrator screens and dehydrate 24 hours.

ASSEMBLY To one side of plate, fill a ring mold with couscous. Gently (with mold still on) cascade vegetables over and around the couscous. Garnish with harissa and flatbread. Remove the ring mold. SERVES 6–8

orange blossom water tart with star anise "ice cream"

During an unforgettable culinary journey through the Atlas Mountains of Morocco with a large group of New York chefs, we made a stop at a country store/café in the middle of the desert. We had just stopped to photograph some camels beside the road and came upon a quaint sandy-looking building a bit off the highway and backed by the breathtaking façade of the mountains and sunset behind it. It had been a long day, and that called for mint tea and Moroccan pastry. Although we had enjoyed several delicious meals during our visit, I will always remember the orange blossom–scented pastries that we were served with our tea. I felt as if I were a character in *The Sheltering Sky,* and that flavor will forever remain with me.

CRUST

2 cups pecan crumbs (process pecans until crumb-like consistency)
$1/4$ teaspoon salt
$1/4$ teaspoon cinnamon
1 teaspoon finely chopped orange zest
2 tablespoons maple syrup
1 tablespoon coconut oil, melted
1 tablespoon date paste

FILLING

3 cups cashews, soaked 1–2 hours
6 tablespoons water
2 tablespoons orange blossom water
$3/4$ cup raw agave
$3/4$ cup coconut oil, melted
$1/2$ cup water
1 teaspoon vanilla extract

$1/2$ teaspoon sea salt
$1/4$ vanilla bean, scraped
2 teaspoons orange zest

"ICE CREAM"

$1/2$ cup cashews, soaked 4–6 hours
$1/2$ cup macadamia nuts, soaked 1–2 hours
$1/2$ cup young coconut meat
$1/2$ cup raw agave
$1^{1}/4$ cups water
$1/2$ vanilla bean, scraped
Pinch sea salt
2 teaspoons ground star anise
$1/2$ cup coconut oil

GARNISH

Ground star anise
Thai basil leaves or spearmint leaves

CRUST Mix ingredients together by hand until well combined. Line one large tart pan or four small ones with plastic wrap. Press dough very thinly into tart shells. Optional: dehydrate 24 hours. Chill crust in freezer for 15–30 minutes before filling.

FILLING Blend all ingredients in a Vita-Mix until very smooth. Fill tart crusts and chill in freezer 3–4 hours until firm. Cut while frozen and keep chilled until ready to serve.

"ICE CREAM" Blend all ingredients in Vita-Mix until very smooth. Pour into an ice cream maker and follow manufacturers instructions.

ASSEMBLY Serve tart with a scoop of "ice cream" and garnish with leaves and star anise on the plates. SERVES 8–10

ginger date flan with mint syrup, sesame brittle, and shaved green pear

Mastering the ability to create varying textures is always a major challenge with raw food; persistence and experimentation can improve this immeasurably. With raw food, I can now approximate versions of flan, panna cotta, and all related desserts with a good amount of success. This flan is a sweet dessert—there is no way around that—but if you like exotic endings to a meal, this one will please.

BRITTLE
$1/2$ cup sesame seeds
$1/4$ cup maple syrup
$1/4$ cup flax meal
Pinch sea salt

FLAN
$1^1/2$ cups coconut meat
1 cup cashews, soaked 1–2 hours
$1/2$ cup raw agave
2 tablespoons minced ginger

$1/4$ cup Irish moss
$1/2$ cup dates, soaked 30 minutes in warm water
   and chopped
1 teaspoon vanilla extract
$1/4$ teaspoon nutmeg

SYRUP
$1/2$ cup mint leaves
$1/2$ cup raw agave

GARNISH
1 green pear, shaved thinly
20 mint leaves

BRITTLE Process all ingredients in a food processor until well combined. Spread very thin on a Teflex sheet and dehydrate 12 hours; remove from Teflex and flip onto a screen and dehydrate another 12 hours. Break into large chunks.

FLAN Blend all ingredients in a Vita-Mix until smooth. Pour into flan molds and refrigerate until set.

SYRUP Blend all ingredients well in Vita-Mix and strain through a fine chinois.

ASSEMBLY Unmold the flans. Set 1 flan on each plate and drizzle mint syrup around each. Top with sesame brittle, shaved pear, and mint leaves. SERVES 4

avocado tartare with tamarind-glazed cherry tomatoes, black sesame pappadam, and curry froth

Raw food fans typically love avocados, and for good reason. They evoke fun, sensuality, richness, and nutrition, and are extremely versatile in food preparation. The idea of doing this dish as a tartare was to awaken our guests' palates with an exotic, but not overpowering, starter during the spice dinner. Although there are many potentially powerful elements to this, they are used in a subtle manner and in such a way that the goal of teasing and awakening the taste buds was successful.

TARTARE
2 ripe avocados, diced
2 tablespoons lime juice
1 teaspoon lime zest
2 tablespoons macadamia nut oil
Salt
Black pepper
2 tablespoons chopped cilantro
1 teaspoon crushed coriander seed
1 jalapeño, minced

PAPPADAM
1 cup flax meal
1 cup chopped yellow squash
1/2 cup chopped coconut meat
1 tablespoon fresh lemon juice
2 cups water
2 tablespoons raw agave
1/2 teaspoon salt
1/2 teaspoon coriander
1/2 teaspoon cumin
1/4 cup black sesame seeds

FROTH
11/2 cups red bell pepper, puréed
2 cups chopped mango
3/4 teaspoon salt
2 tablespoons curry powder
1/2 teaspoon garam masala
1/4 teaspoon paprika
1/4 teaspoon turmeric
1/2 cup cashews, soaked 1–2 hours
2 tablespoons fresh lime juice
3 tablespoons sesame oil
1 teaspoon nama shoyu

TAMARIND-GLAZED CHERRY TOMATOES
1/2 cup halved cherry tomatoes
1 cup dried tamarind, soaked 30 minutes
1/4 cup raw agave
1 teaspoon chili powder
1 teaspoon cayenne
2 tablespoons fresh lime juice
2 tablespoons sesame oil

TARTARE Gently mix all ingredients in a medium bowl. Line soufflé cups with plastic wrap and gently press mixture into cups. Refrigerate 1–2 hours. Unmold directly onto serving dish.

PAPPADAM Blend all ingredients except sesame seeds in a Vita-Mix until smooth. Spread thinly into 3-inch rounds on dehydrator Teflex sheets; sprinkle with black sesame seeds. Dehydrate 5–6 hours, flip, and dehydrate until crisp.

FROTH Blend all ingredients in Vita-Mix until smooth.

TAMARIND-GLAZED CHERRY TOMATOES Dehydrate tomatoes until soft, about 1 hour. Remove seeds from tamarind, push pulp through a coarse strainer, and blend in Vita-Mix with remaining ingredients. When ready to assemble, toss tomatoes with enough tamarind glaze to coat them.

ASSEMBLY Invert tartare on plates and top with tomatoes. Blend froth to create foam and spoon a generous amount of foam around each tartare. Garnish with pappadam.
SERVES 4–6

sweet pea samosas, mint-almond chutney, and pickled lime "yogurt"

My childhood fondness for sweet flavors was ultimately balanced with the introduction of sour, via my experience with Mediterranean, and particularly Sicilian, cooking. *Agrodolce*, which in Italian translates to "sweet and sour," is a great concept, and when used properly, adds a surprise element to food. In this recipe, the sweetness of the peas and the coconut wrapper of the samosas is nicely balanced with the pickled lime yogurt. This is one of my favorite dishes ever to come out of my former restaurant The Plant.

WRAPPERS
2 cups chopped coconut meat
Pinch sea salt
1/2 cup chopped mint leaves

FILLING
1 cup chopped jicama
2 cups raw sweet peas
1 cup macadamia nuts
1/2 cup water
1 teaspoon coriander
1 teaspoon garam masala
1 teaspoon chili powder
1 teaspoon salt
Black pepper to taste
2 tablespoons nutritional yeast
2 tablespoons chopped cilantro
1 tablespoon chopped mint

CHUTNEY
1 1/2 cups almonds, soaked 8–10 hours
1 1/4 cups fresh mint, roughly chopped
1/4 cup orange zest
1/4 cup fresh lemon juice
1/4 cup raw agave
1 teaspoon chili powder
1 cup olive oil
1 teaspoon salt
Black pepper

"YOGURT"
1 1/2 cups cashews, soaked 1–2 hours
1 cup coconut meat
1/2 cup water
1/3 cup fresh lime juice
Zest of 3 limes
1/2 teaspoon salt

GARNISH
Mint leaves

WRAPPERS Blend coconut and salt in a Vita-Mix until very smooth; stir in mint. Spread mixture in a thin layer over 2 dehydrator teflex sheets for 4–5 hours until fully dehydrated. Remove wrappers from sheets, trim edges, and cut into 4 even strips. Store in plastic wrap until ready to use.

FILLING Process jicama in a food processor until well minced. Add peas to gently crush. Set aside. In a Vita-Mix, blend macadamia nuts, water, spices, salt, pepper, and nutritional yeast. Add to pea mixture and check seasoning. Dehydrate 90 minutes, stirring occasionally. Allow to cool, then add cilantro and mint.

Lay coconut wrappers on a work surface. At one of the long ends, place 1 tablespoon of the filling and fold, diagonally, until a full triangular packet is completed. Reserve.

CHUTNEY Pulse-chop almonds in food processor; place in a bowl and set aside. Pulse-chop remaining ingredients in food processor; mix with almonds in bowl.

"YOGURT" Blend all ingredients in a Vita-Mix until smooth.

ASSEMBLY Interlock samosas on individual plates or a platter and spoon a generous amount of "yogurt" over them. Drizzle the chutney around the outside and garnish with mint leaves. YIELDS 16–20

spring vegetables with curry sauce, "rice" with coconut sauce, and banana-ginger raita

Many recipes with spice need at least a moderate amount of heat for their flavors to fully open . . . the process of dehydrating the sauce here provides that effect and helps create a mild rather than bitter or harsh curry, which is often the result of a "raw" underdeveloped sauce. This is a very exotic dish with ginger, curry, and coconut; all evoke a tropical day under a palm tree in the sun.

"RICE"
3 cups chopped jicama
1/2 cup pine nuts
1 teaspoon coriander

COCONUT SAUCE
2 cups coconut meat
3/4 cup coconut water
2 tablespoons raw agave
2 tablespoons fresh lime juice
1/4 teaspoon salt
Pinch cayenne

VEGETABLES
1/2 cup shelled sweet peas
1 cup cherry tomato halves
1 cup sliced shiitake mushrooms
6 stalks asparagus, cut into 11/2-inch lengths
Olive oil
Salt and pepper

CURRY SAUCE
1 cup coconut meat
1/4 cup raw cashews, soaked 1 hour or more

2 tablespoons fresh lime juice
3 tablespoons chopped jalapeño plus seeds to taste
3 scallions, white part and some green
2 tablespoons chopped ginger
1/4 cup grated lemongrass
1/4 cup loosely packed basil leaves
2 teaspoons curry powder, or to taste
1 teaspoon sea salt

RAITA
1/4 cup coconut water
1/4 cup coconut meat
1 semi-ripe banana
3 tablespoons tamarind paste (from pulp)
1/2 teaspoon ground ginger
1 tablespoon fresh lime juice
Pinch sea salt

GARNISH
Curry powder
Fresh mint leaves

"RICE" Pulse all ingredients in a food processor until rice-like consistency is achieved.

COCONUT SAUCE Blend all ingredients in a Vita-Mix until smooth.

VEGETABLES Toss each vegetable separately with olive oil and season with salt and pepper. Dehydrate the sweet peas for 30 minutes, tomatoes for 1 hour, and shiitake and asparagus for 90 minutes.

CURRY SAUCE Blend all ingredients in a Vita-Mix until smooth.

RAITA Blend coconut water and meat together. Chop banana into small dice and toss with tamarind paste. Add remaining ingredients together and mix gently.

ASSEMBLY Combine vegetables with 2/3 of the curry sauce. Combine rice with coconut sauce. In a ring mold, form rice in center of plate. Top with raita. Arrange vegetables around rice and garnish with additional sauce, curry powder, and mint leaves. **SERVES 4–6**

white raisin shiitake dosas, cilantro cream, and ginger-tomato chutney

The first time I had a dosa, at Hampton Chutney in Soho, I wondered where they had been all these years. Dosas are so much fun to eat—and full of exotic tastes. I have always wondered why they aren't more popular. I use this variation whenever I have the opportunity. They are definitely far better when served directly from the dehydrator, still slightly warm, as they tend to be a bit chewy otherwise.

DOSAS
1¹/₂ cups flax meal
1 cup chopped yellow squash
¹/₂ cup chopped coconut meat
1 tablespoon fresh lemon juice
2 cups water
2 tablespoons raw agave
¹/₂ teaspoon salt
1 teaspoon cumin

FILLING
¹/₂ cup golden raisins
¹/₂ cup warm water
¹/₄ cup ginger juice
2 cups sliced shiitake mushrooms
1 teaspoon minced ginger
¹/₄ cup olive oil
Salt and pepper
¹/₄ cup chopped almonds

CHUTNEY
2 cups sun-dried tomatoes, reconstituted
¹/₂ shallot, chopped
2 Roma tomatoes, diced
2 tablespoons fresh lemon juice
¹/₄ cup olive oil
3 tablespoons raw agave
1 tablespoon salt
1 teaspoon chili pepper flakes
¹/₄ cup ginger juice

CREAM
1¹/₂ cups cashews, soaked 1–2 hours
¹/₂ cup coconut meat
¹/₂ cup water
¹/₄ cup lemon juice
¹/₂ teaspoon salt
¹/₄ cup cilantro

GARNISH
¹/₄ cup chopped almonds
Cilantro leaves

DOSAS Blend all ingredients in a Vita-Mix until smooth. Spread thinly into 6- to 7-inch rounds on dehydrator Teflex sheets. Dehydrate 5–6 hours until dry but very pliable.

FILLING Soak raisins in the water with ginger juice. Toss shiitake with minced ginger, olive oil, salt, and pepper, and dehydrate 1 hour. Drain raisins and combine with shiitake and almonds.

CHUTNEY Pulse-chop sun-dried tomatoes and shallot in a food processor. Place mixture in bowl with Roma tomatoes. Blend remaining ingredients in Vita-Mix until smooth; add to bowl. Stir until well combined.

CREAM Blend all ingredients except cilantro in Vita-Mix until smooth and creamy. Add cilantro and blend for a few moments until cilantro is well incorporated. Serve or store in refrigerator 3–4 days.

ASSEMBLY Fill dosas with raisin-shiitake mixture and gently fold closed. Place one dosa on each plate, top with chutney, and drizzle with cream. Garnish with nuts and cilantro. SERVES 4–6

creamy mango pudding, cardamom kulfi, and crispy lime macaroon

Kulfi is an Indian-style ice cream that is richer and creamier than regular ice cream, due to the lack of air that is whipped into traditional ice cream to make it lighter. The milk, traditionally from buffalo, is reduced by at least 50 percent before being incorporated into the recipe. Of course, in our raw version, we simply made a creamier nut-milk base with similar results.

PUDDING
2 cups coconut meat
2 cups chopped mango
1 cup water
$1/2$ cup raw agave
1 cup cashews, soaked 1–2 hours
1 tablespoon vanilla extract
1 tablespoon salt
2 tablespoons coconut oil
$1/2$ teaspoon cinnamon
$1/2$ teaspoon nutmeg

KULFI
$1/4$ cup coconut oil
1 cup coconut meat
$1/4$ cup raw agave
10 white cardamom pods
1 teaspoon rose water

MACAROON
$2^1/4$ cups coconut flakes
2 cups almond crumbs
1 cup almond flour
$1/4$ teaspoon sea salt
$1/4$ cup lime zest
$3/4$ cup maple syrup
$1/2$ cup coconut oil, melted
$1^1/2$ teaspoons vanilla extract

PUDDING Blend in a Vita-Mix and strain through a chinois. Chill, preferably overnight.

KULFI Blend all ingredients in Vita-Mix until smooth.

MACAROON Mix together dry ingredients. Add wet ingredients to dry mixture and mix thoroughly. Spread $1/2$ inch thick onto dehydrator Teflex sheets. Dehydrate 24–48 hours. Cut into desired shapes and transfer to dehydrator screens; —dehydrate another 8–10 hours.

ASSEMBLY Fill a 4-inch ring mold with pudding. Spread a thin layer of kulfi on the top, and garnish with a macaroon.
SERVES 4

apricot "yogurt" cake, sweet cream, pistachio tuiles, and anise syrup

When apricots are in season, buy them! I can have a bowl of several dozen in my home, and they'll never make it past three days. Fresh apricots are such a different temptation than dried, and their sweetness is so mild and intoxicating that you will keep taking another for quite some time before you realize what it is about them that is so addictive.

CAKE
3/4 cup cashews, soaked 1–2 hours
1 cup coconut meat
1 cup dried apricots, reconstituted
6 fresh apricots, pitted and roughly chopped
1/3 cup raw agave
1/4 cup coconut oil
Pinch salt
1/4 teaspoon vanilla extract
1/2 vanilla bean, scraped
Juice of 1/2 lime
1 teaspoon garam masala

CREAM
2 cups cashews, soaked 4 hours
1 cup coconut meat
1 tablespoon vanilla extract
1/2 teaspoon salt
1/2 cup raw agave

TUILES, OPTIONAL
1 1/4 cups flax meal
3/4 cup chopped pear
1/2 cup coconut meat
2 1/4 teaspoons fresh lemon juice
1 cup water
1 cup maple syrup
1/4 teaspoon salt
2 teaspoons vanilla
1 1/2 teaspoons garam masala
1 1/2 teaspoons cinnamon
3 cups pistachios, finely chopped to crumb form

SYRUP
1 cup raw agave
2 teaspoons cinnamon
1/2 teaspoon ground star anise
Pinch salt

CAKE Blend all ingredients in a Vita-Mix until smooth. Line a 10-inch cake pan with plastic wrap. Pour dough into pan. Refrigerate overnight.

CREAM Blend all ingredients in Vita-Mix until smooth.

TUILES Blend all ingredients in Vita-Mix until smooth. Spread thinly over dehydrator Teflex sheets. Dehydrate 5–6 hours until dry but very pliable. Remove from Teflex sheets and shape each round; if needed, use paper clips to secure the edges. Place cones on dehydrator screens and dehydrate another 24 hours until crisp. Remove paper clips.

SYRUP Blend all ingredients in Vita-Mix until smooth.

ASSEMBLY Cut the cake into squares; place a square on a dessert plate, pour anise syrup around edges of cake, and spoon several tablespoons of cream on top of each. Lean tuiles against side of cake. SERVES 4–6

vegetables and grape leaf dolmas with sumac flatbread and cool mint, tahini, and aleppo pepper sauces

Dolma is derived from the Turkish verb *dolmak,* which means "to stuff." It works with a variety of vegetables and fillings, and because I created this recipe during the summer when baby squash and tomatoes were at their peak, this is what I based this on. The many types of baby squash and zucchini gave this dish an extremely interesting presentation—the spices are not classic Turkish, yet the dish took me back to Istanbul.

VEGETABLE DOLMAS
1 cup almond crumbs
2 tablespoons chopped parsley
12 pattypan squash, with centers scooped out and reserved
12 baby zucchini, split, with centers scooped out and reserved
12 cherry tomatoes, halved, with centers scooped out and reserved
3 tablespoons olive oil
1/4 cup fresh lemon juice
Salt and pepper

GRAPE LEAF DOLMAS
3 cups roughly chopped cauliflower
1 cup macadamia nuts, soaked 1–2 hours
1/2 cup olive oil
3 tablespoons nama shoyu
1 teaspoon salt

2 teaspoons garam masala
1 teaspoon coriander
1/2 teaspoon cumin
2/3 cup currants
18 grape leaves

FLATBREAD
1 cup flax meal
1 tablespoon dried basil
1 1/2 teaspoons dried oregano
2 teaspoons sumac, divided, plus more for sprinkling
2 yellow squash, roughly chopped
1 1/2 cups walnuts, soaked 8–10 hours
1 1/2 teaspoons salt
Black pepper
2 pinches cayenne
1/4 cup olive oil
1 shallot, minced
1 tablespoon nutritional yeast
2 tablespoons raw agave
Whole micro-basil leaves

VEGETABLE DOLMAS Pulse the almond crumbs and parsley in a food processor. Add vegetable fillings, olive oil, and lemon juice. Season to taste with salt and pepper, and fill the vegetables with this mixture.

GRAPE LEAF DOLMAS Process cauliflower in food processor to ricelike consistency; place cauliflower in a separate bowl and set aside. Blend remaining ingredients except grape leaves in a Vita-Mix until smooth. Pour over cauliflower and mix until well coated. Spread mixture on dehydrator Teflex

sheets and dehydrate 1–2 hours. Roll grape leaves with equal amounts of filling.

FLATBREAD Place flax meal, basil, and oregano in a medium-size bowl; set aside. Process remaining ingredients except extra sumac and micro-basil leaves in a food processor until smooth. Add to bowl with flax meal and stir until well combined. Spread on Teflex sheets to 1/2 inch thickness; sprinkle with extra sumac and micro-basil. Dehydrate at 115 degrees F for 6–8 hours until almost completely dry

continued on page 140

MINT SAUCE
1/4 cup fresh mint
1/4 cup coconut meat
1/4 cup coconut water
2 tablespoons fresh lime juice
Salt

TAHINI SAUCE
1/3 cup tahini
2 tablespoons fresh lemon juice
2 tablespoons olive oil
Pinch cayenne

1/2 teaspoon cumin
Salt

ALEPPO PEPPER SAUCE
1 cup diced fresh red pepper
1 tablespoon aleppo pepper spice
1/2 cup coconut meat
Salt
2 tablespoons fresh lemon juice
1/4 cup water, as needed

but still a bit pliable. Transfer bread to dehydrator screens and dehydrate 24 hours.

MINT SAUCE Blend all ingredients in Vita-Mix. This sauce should be light green in color and thin with a slight creaminess.

TAHINI SAUCE Blend all ingredients in Vita-Mix until smooth.

ALEPPO PEPPER SAUCE Blend all ingredients in Vita-Mix until smooth, adding water as necessary.

ASSEMBLY Place 2 of each stuffed vegetable on each plate, along with sumac flatbread and grape leaves. Use 1 of each sauce on each of the vegetable dolmas. **SERVES 4–6**

**Do not anticipate trouble
or worry about what
may never happen. Keep in the sunlight.**

—Benjamin Franklin

radiance

The idea of spicy exotic food served in the open air, in close proximity to the sea, is an image that nearly anyone would feel positive about. Maybe it's the symbolic relationship of warm coastal climates to relaxing and eating well, but I have always been drawn to the flavors of sunny countries. The vibrancy of ingredients and sparkling clean flavors combined with a healthy dose of heat is a relentless charm.

A close friend once said to me that he always went to the sea to heal—and I have grown to realize that I am the same, if not in a medical sense, at least emotionally and physically to a large degree. The salty air, the sound of gentle waves, the rocky beaches, and the terrain of oceanfront land all provide a sense of health and, at the same time, exploration. My most positive moments—and my most productive, creative ones—are typically by the sea.

Naturally, the abundance of life, moving water, quick breezes, rapidly changing climates, and proliferation of wildlife and water fowl all combine to create an intoxicating energy that contributes to the cuisine of lands by the sea.

I was fortunate to grow up on a rocky New England coast. Little did I know how that would influence my life and career down the road. Today, I find its presence in nearly every aspect of what I do, physically or spiritually. Life has its way of creating circular paths, regardless of our chosen direction.

Much of my travel has been in the Mediterranean or on the coast of Latin and South America and other water-bordering regions of the United States. All foods have a life source, and I find that those prepared near the sea have more than their ample share. It is not only the ingredients but also the spirit that goes into their preparation as well as the sense of peace when consuming them.

The dishes in this section are recognized for their association with this spirit, for their ability to remind us of beautiful places visited in the past, and for the lifestyle they represent. They are most suitable to a summer afternoon luncheon, a dinner outdoors under the stars, a warm day, a casual celebration—and most of the food experiences we might associate with a slower, relaxing gathering.

caribbean conch chowder

The life of a food lover adds a great deal to one's memory; so often clouded by time and place, we develop taste memories that symbolize our experience with a dish. My first taste of conch was at a beach café in Mexico many years ago. I spent a long day in the sun reading *Tender is the Night,* so immersed in the book that I felt as if I were on the beach next to the divers. After a couple of iced margaritas, the chilled conch was impeccable. I never had it again, but this version succeeded in recapturing that moment for me. Not only did I love the flavor of this chowder, I also loved being transported back to a quieter, relaxing time in my life.

CREAM
1 cup Brazil nuts, soaked 8–12 hours
3 cups water
2 tablespoons olive oil
2 tablespoons fresh lemon juice
1 tablespoon nama shoyu
1 shallot
1 teaspoon nutritional yeast

2 teaspoons salt
Black pepper
$1/2$ teaspoon chili powder
Pinch cayenne

ASSEMBLY
2 cups chopped young Thai coconut meat
$1/2$ cup diced red bell pepper
$1/2$ cup minced celery
2 tablespoons minced scallions

CREAM Blend Brazil nuts and water in a Vita-Mix. Strain through a fine strainer and discard the pulp. Blend this nut milk and the remaining ingredients in Vita-Mix until completely smooth and creamy. Taste for seasoning.

ASSEMBLY Divide the soup among 4 bowls and garnish right before serving with the ingredients listed.

NOTE: When I first served this dish at a Caribbean dinner, we poured the soup inside young coconuts with the flesh still intact. The presentation is always fun, and the fresh tender coconut meat is great when scooped out and eaten with the chowder. SERVES 4–6

roasted sweet pepper soup, basil manti, and hazelnut "yogurt"

Red sweet peppers (longer and thinner skinned than red bell peppers) are ideal for making soups in the summer, when they are sweet and combine well with spices, nuts, and herbs. I was fortunate to have a consulting position in Istanbul many years ago, when I became close friends with the family I was working with, who owned the Borsa Restaurant group. They are the most hospitable people I have ever met and always went out of their way not only to feed me well but also to educate me on their native cuisine. Turkey is one of few countries that produces all of its own food, and the ingredients are impeccable. Manti are dumplings, traditionally filled with lamb and served in a yogurt sauce. As always, we've reinterpreted everything and came up with a dish that was everyone's favorite.

SOUP (2 QUARTS)
1 cup cashews, soaked 1–2 hours
5 cups water
1 cup coconut meat
$3^{1}/2$ teaspoons salt
Black pepper
2 teaspoons fresh lemon juice
1 teaspoon nutritional yeast
2 pinches cayenne pepper
$3/4$ teaspoon Aleppo pepper spice
2 cups red bell pepper pieces, dehydrated 2 hours

WRAPPERS
2 cups coconut meat
$1/2$ cup fresh basil leaves
1 tablespoon water
Pinch salt

FILLING
2 cups roughly chopped portobello mushrooms
$1/2$ cup roughly chopped red onions
Olive oil
Salt
Black pepper
$1/2$ cup cashews, soaked 1–2 hours
1 teaspoon chopped thyme

"YOGURT"
$1^{3}/4$ cups hazelnuts, soaked 1–2 hours
$1/2$ cup coconut meat
$3/4$ cup water
$1/3$ cup fresh lemon juice
$1/4$ teaspoon salt

GARNISH
Chervil

SOUP Blend all ingredients in a Vita-Mix until smooth. Warm in a dehydrator until ready to serve.

WRAPPERS Blend all ingredients in Vita-Mix until very smooth. Using an offset spatula, spread the mixture thinly on dehydrator Teflex sheets and dehydrate at 115 degrees F for 3–4 hours, or until the surface is dry. Carefully flip over and remove from Teflex. Wrappers should be pliable and completely dry. On a flat surface, trim the edges and cut into 9 equal squares.

FILLING Toss portobello mushrooms and onions with olive oil (just to coat), salt, and pepper. Dehydrate 30–40 minutes. Pulse in a food processor with cashews and thyme to chop into small pieces and set aside.

"YOGURT" Blend all ingredients in Vita-Mix until smooth and creamy. Store in refrigerator and bring back to room temperature before serving.

ASSEMBLY Place $1^1/2$ teaspoons of manti filling in center of wrapper. Moisten edges. Gently fold four corners to meet in center. Lightly press. Divide soup among 4 bowls and gently place 2 dumplings in each. Garnish with chervil and spoon a generous amount of "yogurt" into soup. SERVES 4–6

NOTE: These wrappers can be prepared in advance and stored in the refrigerator for quite some time. I have found that they remain fresh for a couple of weeks (perhaps longer, but they never last that long without someone eating them first) and are easily used as a wrapper for anything when you would like to prepare a quick lunch or snack. They should be well sealed in plastic wrap and kept dry. Remove them from the refrigerator at least 20 minutes before handling so that they become more pliable.

spinach and beet ravioli, cashew "ricotta,"
wilted spinach with basil, and wine pear sauce

In my early years with raw food, this same combination of ingredients may have resulted in a raw beet filled with a seasoned cashew purée, but this version is a well-tuned example of how far raw food has progressed. A standard coconut wrapper infused with spinach and beet creates a brilliant color contrast but is also a light, delicious base for the creamy cashew purée, chewy and tangy spinach, and the sweet pear sauce. I found it to be one of the most well-balanced dishes to come from my kitchen, and it is now something I serve whenever I have the opportunity.

RAVIOLI
2 cups chopped coconut meat, divided
2 tablespoons spinach juice
$1/4$ teaspoon salt, divided
2 tablespoons beet juice

"RICOTTA"
$3^1/2$ cups cashews, soaked 1–2 hours
$1/4$ cup fresh lemon juice
$1/2$ cup water
1 cup olive oil
$1^1/2$ teaspoons salt
2 teaspoons nutritional yeast

SAUCE
$2^1/2$ pears, peeled, cored, and chopped
$1/4$ teaspoon salt
$1/4$ cup raw agave
$1/2$ cup white wine

SPINACH
2 quarts torn spinach
1 quart fresh basil leaves
Olive oil
Salt

GARNISH
Fresh basil

RAVIOLI Blend half the coconut with spinach juice and half the salt in a Vita-Mix until very smooth. Spread very thin on dehydrator Teflex sheets and dehydrate 3–4 hours. Repeat the process with the beet version, using the beet juice instead of spinach. Remove from Teflex and trim edges. Cut into 9 squares.

"RICOTTA" Process all ingredients in a food processor 3–5 minutes until smooth.

SAUCE Blend all ingredients in Vita-Mix until smooth. Prior to serving, place in a dehydrator for 20–30 minutes at 115 degrees F to warm.

SPINACH Toss all ingredients in a medium-size bowl. Let sit for 30 minutes in a warm place.

ASSEMBLY Assemble the ravioli by placing 1 teaspoon "ricotta" on half the spinach and half the beet raviolis. Wet corners slightly and press remaining pasta squares on top of the same color wrappers—press tightly.

Spoon sauce onto plates, keeping it away from edges, and place 2 spinach and 2 beet ravioli on each plate. Garnish with wilted spinach and fresh basil. SERVES 4–6

arugula gnocchi, sweet pepper sauce, marinated asparagus, and pine nut "parmesan"

Shortly after beginning my first real restaurant job at the Sicilian restaurant Malvasia, I happened to be in the right place at the right time. The chef, Gennaro Picone, was a master with pasta, and every dish on his menu was outstanding. Most were light, but his gnocchi were rich and delicious. They were a bright green from subtly steamed spinach and were like eating green clouds—they were even good plain and cold, not to mention how they were with the woodsy porcini mushrooms and Gorgonzola cream that he served them with. In the time I worked there, I often tried preparing gnocchi at home, but they were never the same. It takes a very light touch and a lot of practice to make a proper gnocchi, and the creation of this dish certainly held up to the challenge I expected.

GNOCCHI
2 cups chopped jicama, processed in food processor and strained
1 cup cashews, soaked 1–2 hours
3/4 teaspoon sea salt
1/2 teaspoon nutritional yeast
1/3 cup fresh lemon juice
Black pepper
1/4 cup cashew flour
1/2 cup chopped arugula

SAUCE
1 cup cashews, soaked 1–2 hours
1 cup diced red bell pepper, dehydrated 12 hours
1/4 cup coconut meat
1/4 fresh red bell pepper, chopped
1/2 cup olive oil
2 teaspoons salt
Black pepper
2 teaspoons fresh lemon juice
1 pinch cayenne pepper

ASPARAGUS
1/2 bunch asparagus
Olive oil
Salt
Black pepper

"PARMESAN"
(see page 38)

GNOCCHI Mix first 6 ingredients in a large bowl. Blend in batches in a Vita-Mix until very smooth. Place mixture in large bowl and stir in cashew flour and arugula by hand. Shape into gnocchi and gently roll on dehydrator screens to create gnocchi pattern. Place in dehydrator for 2–3 hours or until crust forms around outside. Serve immediately or warm in dehydrator until ready to serve.

SAUCE Blend all ingredients in Vita-Mix until smooth. Warm in dehydrator until ready to serve.

ASPARAGUS Cut the asparagus on a bias into 1½-inch lengths. Toss with olive oil, salt, and pepper. Dehydrate on Teflex sheets for 30–40 minutes.

ASSEMBLY Coat the bottom of the plate with sauce. Place gnocchi on sauce, and garnish with asparagus and "Parmesan." SERVES 4–6

orange-pineapple flan and lime syrup

This Caribbean-influenced dish brings together the classic flavor combination of two sweet ingredients, orange and pineapple, which are offset by the tangy lime syrup. Any citrus and tropical fruit combinations would work well as a substitute in this dish. For example, grapefruit and mango would be a very good choice.

FLAN
1 1/2 cups coconut meat
1 1/4 cups chopped pineapple
1/3 cup orange juice
1/2 cup raw agave
2/3 cup coconut oil
Salt

SYRUP
1 cup raw agave
1/4 cup plus 2 tablespoons fresh lime juice
1 teaspoon lime zest
1/4 teaspoon vanilla extract

FLAN Blend all ingredients in a Vita-Mix until smooth. Pour into plastic-lined ramekins. Refrigerate overnight or freeze 1–2 hours prior to serving. When ready to serve, use an offset spatula to carefully remove flan onto a serving plate.

SYRUP Whisk all ingredients until well combined.

ASSEMBLY Spoon lime syrup over and around flan and serve. SERVES 4–6

salpicao salad with pineapple carpaccio and "fried" jicama

I will readily admit that I was a skeptic when I heard about a staff member's goal of preparing this dish—it sounds quite delicious, but I was curious about the "fried" jicama and the flavor combinations. It worked quite well and goes well beyond a typical salad preparation in terms of its color and variety of tastes and textures. It is a dish that I imagine enjoying with a cool glass of white wine on a South American beach.

DRESSING
$1^1/_2$ cups cashews, soaked 1–2 hours
$3/_4$ cup olive oil
$1/_4$ cup coconut meat
$1/_4$ cup water
1 teaspoon salt
$1/_2$ teaspoon cumin
2 teaspoons fresh lemon juice
2 tablespoons raw agave

VEGETABLES
2 cups thinly sliced shiitake mushrooms
Olive oil
Salt and pepper
2 tablespoons fresh lime juice

$3/_4$ cup green olives, pitted and chopped
1 cup corn
4 cups julienned carrots
$3/_4$ cup raisins, soaked 20 minutes
$1/_4$ cup thinly chopped parsley

JICAMA
4 cups julienned jicama
Olive oil
$1/_2$ teaspoon salt
1 tablespoon nutritional yeast
$1/_3$ cup flax meal

GARNISH
12 pineapple slices ($1/_8$ inch thick)
Parsley sprigs

DRESSING Blend all ingredients in a Vita-Mix until smooth.

VEGETABLES Toss shiitake mushrooms with olive oil, salt, and pepper. Dehydrate on Teflex sheets for 30 minutes. Combine with lime juice and let it sit for 10 minutes. Mix with remaining ingredients.

JICAMA Squeeze jicama of liquid. Toss with olive oil and mix with remaining ingredients. Place on dehydrator screens and dehydrate 36 hours.

ASSEMBLY Mix vegetables with dressing. Drain excess liquid. Place 3 pineapple slices in the center of each plate, overlapping each other. Top with dressed vegetables. Gently place jicama on top and garnish with parsley sprigs. SERVES 4–6

creamy eggplant and hummus cream in almond tart shells with green olive tapenade

The first taste of this dish took me on a culinary journey backward around the world. My first sous chef was Malcolm Johnson, one of a few mad scientists that I would have the good fortune of working with over the years. He introduced me to this green olive tapenade at my first restaurant and it has followed me over the years, first with tuna tartare, then with a charcoal grilled vegetable pizza, and now this raw dish. The almond crust is purely Moroccan, the Hummus very much from the Eastern Mediterranean—and the dish as a whole, quite New York.

TART SHELLS
1 cup almonds, processed to crumb form
1/4 cup cashew flour
1 teaspoon salt
1 1/2 teaspoons nutritional yeast
1 tablespoon olive oil
2 tablespoons water
1 1/2 teaspoons cumin

CREAM
1/2 cup cashews, soaked 1–2 hours
1/4 cup macadamia nuts, soaked 1–2 hours
1 tablespoon fresh lemon juice
2 teaspoons olive oil

4 tablespoons tahini
1/2 teaspoon salt
4 tablespoons water
1 clove garlic

TAPENADE
1/2 cup pitted green olives
2 tablespoons fresh lemon juice
3 tablespoons olive oil
Pinch anise seed

EGGPLANT
1 large eggplant, chopped
2 tablespoons olive oil
Pinch salt
Pinch pepper
1 teaspoon garam masala

TART SHELLS Mix all ingredients in a bowl with hands. Use your fingers to press into plastic-lined individual tart shells (3 1/2- to 4-inch diameter with removable bottoms) and dehydrate overnight. Carefully remove the crusts from the shells, place them back on the dehydrator screen, and continue dehydrating until slightly crisp.

CREAM Blend all ingredients in a Vita-Mix until completely smooth. Store in the refrigerator and bring back to room temperature before serving.

TAPENADE Blend in Vita-Mix until smooth.

EGGPLANT Toss eggplant with olive oil, salt, pepper, and garam masala. Dehydrate until soft.

ASSEMBLY Place the tart shell on the plate and fill with the cream. Top with the eggplant and drizzle with the tapenade.
SERVES 4–6

summer squash pancakes with garlic flower "yogurt," sweet tomato jam, and crisp fennel

One of the luxuries of working with raw food is that I can occasionally dream up a dish that should be impossible to make. But experimentation always seems to defy the impossible—this dish fits that model. The flavors remind me of summer and of the Mediterranean. It may have even been initially inspired by a Socca recipe that I used to love making and eating with a garlicky, tahini yogurt purée. The importance of this dish, like so many others we prepare, lies entirely in the use of the best ingredients.

MACADAMIA PURÉE
1 cup macadamia nuts, soaked 2 hours
3/4 teaspoon lemon zest
1/4 cup water
1/4 shallot, peeled
1/4 clove garlic
2 tablespoons nutritional yeast
Pinch salt
Pinch cayenne

PANCAKES (YIELDS 9)
1/2 pound yellow squash, grated
1/2 pound green squash, grated
Pinch salt
1/2 cup flax meal
2 tablespoons olive oil
2 tablespoons water
1 cup finely chopped green onions
1/4 cup chopped fresh dill
1/4 cup chopped fresh parsley
1 teaspoon dried tarragon
1 teaspoon sea salt
1/2 teaspoon black pepper
1/4 cup Macadamia Purée (see above)

1/4 cup Pine Nut "Parmesan" (see page 38)
1/2 cup chopped walnuts

"YOGURT"
1 3/4 cups cashews, soaked 1–2 hours
1/2 cup coconut meat
3/4 cup water
1/3 cup fresh lemon juice
1/4 teaspoon salt
4 garlic scapes

JAM
1 cup sun-dried tomatoes, reconstituted
1/4 shallot, chopped
1/2 Roma tomato, diced
1 tablespoon fresh lemon juice
2 tablespoons olive oil
2 1/4 teaspoons raw agave
1/4 tablespoon salt
1/4 teaspoon chili pepper flakes

ASSEMBLY
4 cups spinach
Olive oil
Salt and pepper
Fennel bulb

MACADAMIA PURÉE Blend all ingredients in a Vita-Mix until very smooth and creamy.

PANCAKES Toss squashes in salt and place in a chinois for 30 minutes. Squeeze dry with hands and place in a large bowl. Mix flax meal, olive oil, and water in a bowl and add to squashes. Add remaining ingredients to bowl and mix well with hands. Drop into 3-inch rounds on Teflex sheets and dehydrate until crisp on the outside, about 4–5 hours.

"YOGURT" Blend all ingredients in Vita-Mix until smooth and creamy. Store in the refrigerator; warm in dehydrator for 1–2 hours before serving.

JAM Pulse-chop sun-dried tomatoes and shallot in a food processor. Place mixture in a bowl with diced Roma tomato. Blend remaining ingredients in Vita-Mix until smooth and add to bowl. Stir until well combined. Store in refrigerator; warm in dehydrator for 1–2 hours before serving.

ASSEMBLY Toss the spinach with olive oil, salt, and pepper, and place in a bowl; cover with plastic wrap. Dehydrate 30 minutes. Shave the fennel bulb and toss in a bit of salt. Make a bed of the wilted spinach on each plate. Place 2 pancakes per person atop spinach, one overlapping the other. Drizzle with warm yogurt and spoon warm jam on the side. Garnish with the shaved fennel. **SERVES 4–6**

golden and green cannelloni with sun-dried tomato–ginger marinara, mint-basil pistachio pesto, green zebra tomatoes, and pine nut and black truffle "ricotta"

The first raw food dish (or at least, the first successful raw food dish) that I ever created was a green zebra tomato lasagna that I designed for my first raw food menu. There was never a single evening that it wasn't the best-selling dish on the menu, which lies in the fact that it offers familiar flavors in a unique form. Raw food can often be intimidating, especially for those who have never tried it, and the components of this dish resemble a welcoming gesture—tomato sauce, pesto, ricotta, tomatoes. They work together, we've all tried them, and the dish is full flavored.

CANNELLONI
1 golden zucchini
2 green zucchini
Olive oil
Salt
2 green zebra tomatoes, sliced

"RICOTTA"
2 cups pine nuts, soaked 1–2 hours
2 tablespoons nutritional yeast
1/4 cup fresh lemon juice
2 tablespoons black truffle oil
1/4 cup water
1/2 teaspoon salt
2 tablespoons chopped fresh thyme
2 tablespoons chopped scallions

PESTO
1/2 cup packed fresh basil leaves
1/2 cup packed fresh mint leaves
1/4 cup pistachios
1/3 cup olive oil
1/2 teaspoon salt
Pinch black pepper

MARINARA
1 1/2 cups sun-dried tomatoes, soaked 1 hour
1/2 Roma tomato, roughly chopped
1/4 shallot, chopped
1 tablespoon lemon juice
1/4 cup olive oil
2 teaspoons agave
1 1/2 teaspoons salt
1/4 cup ginger juice
Pinch dried chili pepper flakes

ASSEMBLY
Olive oil
Fresh basil leaves or lavender sprigs

CANNELLONI Using a mandoline, cut the zucchini lengthwise into very thin slices. Brush slices with olive oil and sprinkle with a little salt.

"RICOTTA" Pulse nuts in a food processor to break up. Add yeast, lemon juice, oil, and water; blend until smooth. Add salt, thyme, and scallions; pulse until well combined. Store in the refrigerator and bring back to room temperature before serving.

PESTO Place all ingredients in food processor and process until chunky. Store in the refrigerator; bring back to room temperature before serving.

MARINARA Squeeze water from sun-dried tomatoes and place all ingredients in food processor. Process until smooth. Store in refrigerator; bring back to room temperature before serving.

ASSEMBLY Overlap 2 green zucchini slices flat on a work surface, with the ends facing you. Place 2 tablespoons "ricotta" close to the near end; top with 2 tablespoons marinara sauce, 1 tablespoon pesto, and green zebra tomatoes. Roll carefully 3 times, forming a rectangle, and place on the plate. Form gently with hands to shape it. Repeat the same steps with the golden zucchini. Place two green cannelloni and one yellow on each plate. Drizzle with olive oil and garnish with basil or lavender. **SERVES 4–6**

pine nut tartlet, basil "crème fraîche," and sweet tomatoes

I was ready to give up on this dish at one point due to its delicacy—but I pursued it relentlessly and will be forever grateful. It's actually an easy dish to make but should only be attempted when you can find small, fresh, sweet tomatoes at their peak. This remains a recipe that was so clean and vivid that I can easily taste it as I think back to the day I first had it. The variations that are possible for this dish are endless, from doing a different herb or green cream, to the large possibilities of fresh vegetables it could be topped with, ranging from summer squash, fava beans, sweet marinated peas, and radishes.

TART SHELLS
1 cup pine nuts, processed to crumb form
$1/4$ cup almond flour
$1/4$ teaspoon salt
$1/2$ teaspoon nutritional yeast
1 tablespoon olive oil
2 tablespoons water

"CRÈME FRAÎCHE"
$1^1/2$ cups cashews, soaked 1–2 hours
$1/2$ cup water

$3/4$ cup fresh lemon juice
2 teaspoons nutritional yeast
$1/4$ cup fresh basil

TOMATOES
1 pint baby heirloom tomatoes, halved
3 tablespoons olive oil
Pinch salt

GARNISH
Micro basil sprigs

TART SHELLS Place all ingredients in a bowl and combine using your hands. Use your fingers to press into plastic-lined individual tart shells ($3^1/2$- to 4-inch diameter, with removable bottoms) and dehydrate overnight. Carefully remove the crusts from the shells, place them back in the dehydrator, and continue dehydrating until slightly crisp.

"CRÈME FRAÎCHE" Blend all ingredients in a Vita-Mix until smooth and creamy. Store in the refrigerator until firm.

TOMATOES Toss tomatoes with olive oil and salt.

ASSEMBLY Place the tart shell on a plate and fill with the "crème fraîche." Top with baby tomatoes and garnish with micro basil sprigs. **SERVES 4–6**

caldo verde, jicama broth, eggplant bacon, marinated chard, and garlic and onion bread

Caldo Verde is considered by many to be Portugal's national dish. It is comforting, satisfying, and nutritious. I can easily imagine choosing this over a more traditional chicken soup when a bit under the weather. I'm not sure that this version is as familiar in Portugal, but we loved the interpretation.

BROTH
1 cup cashews, soaked 1–2 hours
4 cups jicama
1 quart water
$1/2$ cup olive oil
1 tablespoon sea salt
Black pepper
$1/2$ teaspoon nutritional yeast
1 clove garlic
2 shallots, peeled

EGGPLANT BACON

MARINADE
1 tablespoon sea salt
$1/2$ dried chipotle chile, soaked
$1/2$ cup soaking water from chipotle chile
2 tablespoons maple syrup
2 tablespoons olive oil
2 tablespoons nama shoyu
2 tablespoons apple cider vinegar
1 teaspoon chili powder
$1/2$ teaspoon paprika

$1/2$ teaspoon cumin
Black pepper
Pinch cayenne

EGGPLANT
1 medium eggplant, diced
Salt

CHARD
2 cups chard chiffonade
Olive oil
Salt

BREAD (YIELDS 1 SHEET)
6 cups peeled and chopped sweet Vidalia onions
2 tablespoons chopped garlic
1 cup ground sunflower seeds
1 cup flax meal
$1/2$ cup olive oil
2 teaspoons sea salt
1 tablespoon dried oregano plus more for sprinkling
Black pepper

ASSEMBLY
4 small acorn squash

BROTH Blend all ingredients in a Vita-Mix, store in the refrigerator, and warm in a dehydrator 1–2 hours before serving.

MARINADE Blend all ingredients in Vita-Mix until smooth.

EGGPLANT Toss eggplant with salt and let sit to drain. Squeeze excess liquid. Toss with marinade and let marinate 2–3 hours. Dehydrate 1–2 hours.

CHARD Toss chard with olive oil and salt. Dehydrate in a bowl covered with plastic wrap for 30 minutes.

BREAD Put onions and garlic in a food processor and process into small pieces (but not mush); place in a bowl. Add remaining ingredients and mix well. Spread on Teflex sheets about $1/4$ inch thick and sprinkle with a bit more dried oregano. Place in a dehydrator for 6 hours. Cut into 2 x 3-inch rectangles, then transfer to screens and dehydrate 4 hours more, or until dry and crispy.

ASSEMBLY Cut and save top of squash to use as a lid, if desired. Scoop out filling and pour in broth. Top with chard and eggplant. Serve with bread. SERVES 4–6

shiitake moqueca and coconut "rice"

Moqueca has a long history with our kitchen—my first job as a chef was with a Brazilian restaurant company, and the owners, in their efforts to educate me about their native cuisine, sent me to Rio de Janeiro to learn how to prepare many of their classics, including this great dish. One of my recent sous chefs is also from Rio, and this recipe is her version—far more authentic than mine and quite delicious.

"RICE"
4 cups peeled and roughly chopped jicama
$1/2$ cup coconut meat
2 tablespoons coconut water
$1^1/2$ teaspoons raw agave
$1^1/2$ teaspoons fresh lime juice
$1/4$ teaspoon salt
1 teaspoon coriander
1 pinch cayenne

MOQUECA SAUCE
$1/2$ red onion, chopped
$1^1/2$ tomatoes, seeded and diced
$1/4$ bunch cilantro
1 tablespoon green onion
1 tablespoon parsley
$1/3$ cup carrot juice

$2/3$ cup coconut milk ($1/2$ cup coconut meat and $1/4$ cup water)
$1/2$ teaspoon salt
1 teaspoon cayenne pepper
Black pepper

MUSHROOMS
2 cups thinly sliced shiitake mushrooms
Olive oil
Salt and pepper

TOMATOES
2 cups cherry tomatoes
Olive oil
Salt and pepper
$1/4$ cup finely chopped cilantro

GARNISH
Cilantro

"RICE" Process jicama in a food processor until a rice-like consistency is achieved. Press out excess liquid with a cheesecloth or through a sieve. Place in a medium-size bowl and set aside. Blend remaining ingredients in a Vita-Mix until smooth and creamy. Add to jicama and combine well. Store in the refrigerator until ready to serve. Bring back to room temperature before serving.

MOQUECA SAUCE Blend all ingredients in Vita-Mix. Set aside.

MUSHROOMS Toss mushrooms with olive oil, salt and pepper. Place on Teflex sheets and dehydrate 30–45 minutes.

TOMATOES Toss tomatoes with olive oil, salt, and pepper. Place on Teflex sheets and dehydrate 30–45 minutes.

ASSEMBLY Place $1/4$ cup coconut rice off center of plate and top with cilantro. Pour sauce on plate, top with shiitake mushrooms, and garnish with tomatoes and cilantro.
SERVES 4–6

brigadeiro, pudim de leite, and canjica "ice cream"

This is another dish from a Brazilian dinner I once hosted. It was colorful, vibrant, and, of course, fun. The sake caipirinhas also helped. When one is looking for comfort food, I find that the most satisfying desserts are either very simple and one dimensional or offer a variety of preparations in small portions. That is essentially my philosophy of food, especially raw food in general, but more so with dessert. This was fun to eat, and each component was entirely unique, but they worked together extremely well.

BRIGADEIRO

LAYER CAKE
2^1/$_4$ cups fine cashew flour (passed through a tami)
1^1/$_2$ cups cocoa powder
^{1}/$_4$ teaspoon salt
Pinch cinnamon
^{1}/$_2$ cup raw agave
^{3}/$_4$ cup water
^{1}/$_4$ teaspoon vanilla extract

TRUFFLES
^{1}/$_2$ cup raw cacao powder
2 cups cashews, soaked 4–6 hours
^{1}/$_2$ cup coconut oil
1 teaspoon vanilla extract
^{1}/$_2$ teaspoon salt
^{3}/$_4$ cup raw agave
^{1}/$_4$ cup mesquite pod meal

CHOCOLATE SAUCE
1^1/$_4$ cups raw agave
^{1}/$_2$ cup raw cacao powder
2 tablespoons carob powder
^{1}/$_4$ teaspoon vanilla
Pinch salt
^{1}/$_2$ cup coconut oil

PUDIM DE LEITE
1 cup cashews, soaked 1–2 hours
^{3}/$_4$ cup fresh young Thai coconut meat
^{1}/$_2$ cup raw carrageenan
6 tablespoons raw agave
^{1}/$_4$ teaspoon sea salt
^{3}/$_4$ teaspoon nutritional yeast
2 pinches turmeric
^{1}/$_4$ teaspoon cinnamon

LAYER CAKE Mix together dry ingredients in a large bowl. Add remaining ingredients and mix well with hands. Line a pan (you can use a half sheet tray) with parchment paper. Press the batter into a 1-inch layer. Dehydrate in bottom of dehydrator overnight. Flip onto cutting board and trim edges. Place on dehydrator screens and dehydrate another 4–6 hours.

TRUFFLES Blend all ingredients except mesquite pod meal in a Vita-Mix. Place in a bowl and mix in meal with hands. Place in the freezer 1–2 hours. Divide the recipe in 2.

CHOCOLATE SAUCE Blend all ingredients in Vita-Mix until smooth.

PUDIM DE LEITE Blend all ingredients in a Vita-Mix until completely smooth. Pour into lined ramekins and refrigerate.

continued on page 170

CARAMEL SAUCE
1 cup raw agave
1/4 teaspoon sea salt
1/4 teaspoon cinnamon

"ICE CREAM"
1 cup cashews, soaked 1–2 hours
1/2 cup coconut meat
1/2 cup raw agave
1 1/2 cups water
1 tablespoon vanilla extract
Pinch sea salt

1/2 cup coconut oil
1/4 teaspoon cloves
1 3/4 teaspoons cinnamon
1/2 cup dried coconut flakes
1 cup chopped young Thai coconut meat

ASSEMBLY
1 cup cacao nibs
1/4 cup prunes, soaked in 1/4 cup water and 1/4 cup raw agave
Mint sprigs

CARAMEL SAUCE Blend ingredients in Vita-Mix for 20 seconds. Chill in freezer 2 hours.

"ICE CREAM" Blend all ingredients except chopped Thai coconut meat in Vita-Mix until very smooth. Pour into an ice cream maker, add coconut meat, and follow manufacturer's instructions.

ASSEMBLY Roll 1/2 the truffle recipe into small truffles. Coat with cacao nibs and set aside. Divide the layer cake in 3 even layers. Take 1/3 of the other 1/2 of the truffle recipe and spread over 1 layer of the cake. Cover with the other cake layer and repeat process two more times. Cut cake into 3 x 1/2-inch rectangles. Place 1 rectangle on a plate, pour 2 tablespoons chocolate sauce over the top and garnish with 2 truffles. Place 1 Pudim de Leite next to brigadeiro cake, pour caramel sauce over the top, and garnish with prunes. Place a ball of "ice cream" on the side and garnish with a mint sprig. **SERVES 4–6**

the magic of mesquite

One of the great benefits of a raw food lifestyle, outside the obvious ones, can be found in the multitude of **lesser-known ingredients** that are brought into the preparation of the food. Many of them have incredible flavor and nutritional value, and mesquite is a wonderful example. It has a malted, smoky, caramel flavor that is subtle yet **hauntingly delicious with crackers,** desserts, and other earthy preparations. I haven't produced the dish yet, but I am very interested to experiment with mesquite and wild or exotic mushrooms. In addition to its taste, mesquite is very **high in protein, calcium, magnesium, iron, and more.** An additional benefit that the use of mesquite provides is that as it becomes more popular, fewer of the mesquite forests will be harvested and will ultimately be far more sustainable.

creamy sage-pumpkin "risotto" with wild mushrooms

Another dish inspired by an Italian classic—one bold chef created the idea of adding crushed Amaretti cookies, the ones that come in the bright red packaging and are seasoned with the delicious Amaretto di Saronno, to ravioli of pumpkin. It breaks up the monotonous creamy texture of the dish and provides a surprisingly pleasant sweet element. This variation uses that combination with a risotto version.

"RISOTTO"
4 cups peeled and roughly chopped jicama
1¹/2 cups peeled, chopped, and seeded fresh pumpkin
3 tablespoons extra-virgin olive oil
1/2 cup cashews, soaked 1–2 hours
6 tablespoons water
3/4 teaspoon sea salt
1¹/2 teaspoons raw agave
2 tablespoons fresh sage

WILD MUSHROOMS
1¹/2 cups stemmed and roughly chopped (into 1/2-inch pieces) portobello mushrooms
1¹/2 cups stemmed and roughly chopped (into 1/2-inch pieces) cremini mushrooms
3 tablespoons extra-virgin olive oil
3/4 teaspoon sea salt

Black pepper to taste
1¹/2 teaspoons chopped fresh rosemary
1¹/2 teaspoons chopped fresh thyme

AMARETTI
2 cups coarse almond flour (soaked and dehydrated almonds that are processed and sifted through a fine tamis or strainer—the coarse flour remains unsifted)
1/2 teaspoon almond extract
2 tablespoons date paste
1/2 cup maple syrup powder
1/2 cup coconut butter
Pinch sea salt

GARNISH
8 fresh sage leaves

"RISOTTO" Process jicama in a food processor until ricelike consistency is achieved (do not overprocess). Press out excess liquid with a cheesecloth or through a sieve; place in a medium-size bowl and set aside. Pulse pumpkin in food processor with olive oil; add to jicama rice. Blend remaining ingredients in a Vita-Mix until smooth and creamy. Add to jicama-and-pumpkin mixture and combine well. Optional: cover bowl with plastic wrap and warm in dehydrator at 118 degrees F for 1–2 hours.

WILD MUSHROOMS Toss all ingredients together in a medium-size bowl. Spread mushroom mixture in a small pan and place in the bottom of a dehydrator at 118 degrees F for 20–30 minutes.

AMARETTI Combine all ingredients well. Spoon tablespoon rounds of the dough onto dehydrator sheets, pressing down slightly. Dehydrate 24 hours until mostly crisp on the outside. Allow to cool.

ASSEMBLY Divide the risotto among 4–6 plates. Spoon ¼ cup mushrooms over the risotto on each serving plate. Crumble amaretti over mushrooms. Garnish with fresh sage, if desired. SERVES 4–6

red pepper almond romesco dumplings
with marinated dandelion greens, frozen basil "butter," and green olive–preserved lemon relish

Spanish food has become so creative of late that there are literally no boundaries to its preparation, provided that the flavors are somewhat grounded in tradition. This preparation is an excellent example of remaining pure with a classical flavor combination while taking full liberty with technique and form. The essence of the dish is strictly Mediterranean.

DUMPLING WRAPPERS
2 cups young coconut meat
Pinch salt
2 tablespoons red pepper juice

ROMESCO
8 red bell peppers
6 tomatoes
$1/4$ cup olive oil, divided
1 teaspoon salt, divided
Black pepper
2 large garlic cloves
$1/3$ cup almonds
2 teaspoons chili powder
Pinch cayenne
1 teaspoon paprika
2 tablespoons apple cider vinegar
$1^1/2$ cups finely chopped hazelnuts, soaked for 4 hours and dehydrated overnight

DANDELION GREENS
2 cups trimmed dandelion greens
3 tablespoons olive oil
Salt and pepper to taste
2 tablespoons fresh lemon juice

BASIL "BUTTER"
3 cups olive oil, frozen
$1/2$ cup chopped fresh basil
$1^1/2$ teaspoons salt

RELISH
$1/2$ cup finely chopped preserved lemon
3 tablespoons lemon zest
$1/2$ cup fresh lemon juice
$1/2$ teaspoon black pepper
$1/2$ cup olive oil
$1/4$ cup raw agave
$2/3$ cups diced green olives

DUMPLING WRAPPERS Blend all ingredients in a Vita-Mix and spread thin on Teflex sheets and dehydrate 2–3 hours, until firm but still pliable. Trim edges and cut into 9 squares.

ROMESCO Chop bell peppers and tomatoes; place in separate bowls and toss with half of the olive oil, half the salt, and pepper; spread on dehydrator screens and dehydrate 4–5 hours. In a food processor, place garlic, almonds, chili powder, cayenne, paprika, remaining salt, additional pepper, vinegar, and remaining olive oil, and pulse. Add bell peppers and tomatoes; process 15–20 seconds; place in a large bowl and stir in hazelnuts.

DANDELION GREENS Toss all ingredients in a bowl and set aside to marinate 1 hour.

BASIL "BUTTER" Blend all ingredients and run in an ice cream machine according to manufacturer's instructions; freeze overnight.

RELISH Blend $1/2$ the preserved lemon, the lemon zest, lemon juice, black pepper, olive oil, and agave. Stir in remaining $1/4$ cup chopped preserved lemon and diced olives.

ASSEMBLY Fill the dumpling wrappers with romesco and fold into beggars purses or in desired dumpling shape. Warm in dehydrator.

Pour a couple tablespoons of relish on plates and top with dumplings. Place marinated greens to the side and top them with a teaspoon of frozen basil butter. SERVES 4–6

> *"The greatest revolution of our generation is the discovery that human beings, by changing the inner attitudes of their minds, can change the outer aspects of their lives."*
>
> —William James

revolution

Revolution is something that we, as chefs working with raw organic food, deal with on a daily basis. We are in the midst of one, whether we speak of it or not. A revolution is a turn, a rotation, a change of events that is hopefully (and often) leading to improved conditions. Fortunately, we are blessed with countless sources of superior organic products to prepare our meals with. On the other hand, the food supply chain is riddled with genetically modified ingredients that are shipped from afar, treated with massive amounts of pesticides, and bear little more than a passing resemblance to the fruit or vegetable that they are attempting to imitate. There is a large and growing diversity with how we eat. I see this as a positive sign in many ways, given that the factions at least exist—there is resistance, and ultimately (or at least hopefully) wise choices will prevail.

We embrace revolution for the positive change it may often bring—that is not always the case, but it certainly offers passion, energy, and choice. Many of my dishes are inspired by countries that have been through everything from prosperity, hardship, and struggle in the face of revolution—there is always a sense of pride and thankfulness following such a struggle. It may be our own ability to romanticize history, but we often find that any kitchen becomes most inspired by the foods of these nations—meaningful cuisine with a long history and sensibility—foods that, when prepared in a modern kitchen, become very modern and yet still retain the charm of old-world cuisine.

Revolutions accelerate change, and as change relates to food today, that acceleration is necessary. A staid approach, ignoring the obvious signals from every direction, may lead to peril of one degree or another, whereas the old adage "change is good" has never been more appropriate. We love the idea of fighting for truth, living for health, reaching for meaning, and, most of all, preparing great meals. Let us all forge that path.

The recipes in this chapter embrace revolutionary intellect in the culinary world.

empanada de espinaca y salsa de tomate: empanada with spinach, tomato relish, and cilantro-mint purée

Cuban empanadas are usually filled with seasoned meats. Of course, that won't happen with raw foods, but the concept remains intact. I like serving empanadas as a filled pastry—a casual bite or light meal with a salad. The cilantro-mint purée is an important element in this recipe, as they otherwise may be a bit dry.

PASTRY
3/4 cup flax meal
3 cups corn kernels
1 cup water
2 tablespoons olive oil
2 teaspoons cumin
1/2 small red onion, roughly chopped
1 clove garlic
3/4 teaspoon salt
1 tablespoon fresh lime juice
Pinch cayenne

FILLING
3 cups pine nuts, soaked 1–2 hours
3 tablespoons fresh lemon juice
1 teaspoon salt
3/4 teaspoon nutritional yeast
2 whole scallions

SPINACH
1 quart torn spinach
Olive oil to coat
Salt

RELISH
2 cups finely diced tomatoes
1/4 cup finely diced onions
1 tablespoon olive oil
1/4 cup chopped parsley
2 teaspoons dried oregano
1 tablespoon fresh lime juice
1 teaspoon lime zest

PURÉE
1 cup fresh cilantro
1 cup fresh mint
1 cup olive oil
Salt

GARNISH
Cilantro sprigs

PASTRY Set flax meal aside. Place remaining ingredients in a food processor and blend until smooth. Stir in flax meal. Spread batter onto Teflex sheets in 3-inch circles and dehydrate at 118 degrees F for about 3–4 hours, or until able to flip. Flip rounds onto dehydrator screens and place another screen on top to hold rounds in place; dehydrate an additional 45–60 minutes, or until they are dry but still pliable.

FILLING Process all ingredients except scallions in food processor until smooth. Add scallions and pulse until they have broken up and are well combined. Store in a container in the refrigerator.

SPINACH Toss all ingredients in a medium-size bowl. Let sit 30 minutes or cover with plastic wrap and dehydrate 20 minutes.

RELISH Mix all ingredients in a large bowl.

PURÉE Blend all ingredients in a Vita-Mix until smooth.

ASSEMBLY Spread filling on the side of pastry that is completely dry; top with spinach. Fold pastry in half over filling and secure edges tightly by pressing with the tines of a fork. You may need to wet edges with water before pressing with fork to secure well. Place back on dehydrator screens and dehydrate 15–20 minutes until the outside is completely dry. Place empanadas on the plate and drizzle with purée. Serve with the tomato relish on the side and garnish with cilantro sprigs. **SERVES 4–6**

hallacas vegetarianas: vegetable tamales with tomato-chile sauce

These tiny tamales, wrapped in a strand of corn dyed with beet juice, are so charming that they would be delicious filled with air—yet, the filling has a very silky body and deep flavor that is surprising, given the lack of heavy fats or dairy.

FILLING
1 quart corn, divided
1^1/4 cups minced tomatoes
1^1/2 cups minced red bell pepper
6 tablespoons sun-dried tomatoes, soaked
1^1/4 cups pine nuts, soaked 1–2 hours
1^1/4 cups cashews, soaked 1–2 hours
1 teaspoon sea salt
^{3}/4 teaspoon nutritional yeast
2 tablespoons minced red onion
2 tablespoons stemmed and chopped fresh cilantro
1 clove garlic, peeled and minced
^{3}/4 cup fresh lime juice

SAUCE
2 cups sun-dried tomatoes, soaked 1 hour
1 ancho chile, soaked 10–15 minutes
1 Roma tomato, diced

^{1}/2 shallot, chopped
2 tablespoons fresh lemon juice
^{1}/4 cup olive oil
4 teaspoons raw agave
2 teaspoons salt
Pinch chile pepper flakes

"SOUR CREAM"
1 cup cashews, soaked 1–2 hours
^{1}/2 cup water
^{1}/4 cup olive oil
4^1/2 teaspoons fresh lemon juice
^{3}/4 teaspoon salt

ASSEMBLY
12–18 corn husks
1 cup beet juice
Corn husk "strings" (strands torn from ends of husks
Ancho chile powder

FILLING Place 2 cups corn, the tomatoes, and the red bell pepper in a bowl; set aside. In a food processor, blend the remaining corn and ingredients until very smooth. Pour into the bowl with corn, tomatoes, and red bell pepper, and mix well with hands. Store in refrigerator.

SAUCE Squeeze water from sun-dried tomatoes and ancho chile. Place all ingredients in a Vita-Mix and blend until smooth. Store in refrigerator.

"SOUR CREAM" Blend all ingredients in Vita-Mix until completely smooth. Store in refrigerator.

ASSEMBLY Tear 24–36 strings from corn husks and place in a bowl with beet juice. Place strings on dehydrator screens for 20 minutes to dry. Soak corn husks in water 30 minutes and dry well. Place 2–3 tablespoons tamale filling in the middle of each husk and tie both edges with strings. Place 3 tamales on each plate. Serve with sauce and "sour cream." Sprinkle with ancho chile powder. SERVES 4–6

cornbread bruschetta with white truffle "sour cream" and spiced tomatoes

I love the combination of high/low cuisine—rustic food combined with an elegant ingredient or two. Several years ago, I opened a restaurant, Monzu, which was named for the French chefs who occupied Sicily's kitchens when Napoleon's troops invaded the region. The resulting French approach to traditional Italian cooking brought some interesting contrasts. In my own cuisine, if I were still cooking on a regular basis, I'd love a baked potato with fresh black truffle.

BRUSCHETTA
1 cup flax meal
1 tablespoon dried oregano
2 cups fresh corn kernels
$1^1/_3$ cups walnuts, soaked 8–10 hours
1 tablespoon sea salt
$^1/_2$ teaspoon black pepper
$^1/_4$ cup olive oil
$^1/_2$ shallot, minced
1 tablespoon nutritional yeast
2 tablespoons raw agave nectar
1 tablespoon fresh lemon juice
1 tablespoon minced jalapeño
1 teaspoon ancho chile powder

"SOUR CREAM"
1 cup cashews, soaked 1–2 hours
$^1/_2$ cup water
$^1/_4$ cup olive oil

2 tablespoons fresh lemon juice
$^1/_2$ teaspoon salt
3 tablespoons white truffle oil

TOMATO
1 tablespoon chopped cilantro
1 tablespoon nama shoyu
1 tablespoon olive oil
3 tomatoes, seeded and diced
1 tablespoon minced shallots
1 tablespoon chopped chipotle peppers, soaked 1 hour
Salt and pepper to taste
3 tablespoons julienned basil

ASSEMBLY
$^1/_4$ cup basil leaves
Fresh black pepper

BRUSCHETTA Place flax meal in a medium-size bowl; set aside. Process remaining ingredients in a food processor until smooth. Add to bowl with flax meal and stir until well combined. Spread on Teflex sheets in desired shape to $^1/_2$-inch thickness. Dehydrate at 115 degrees F for 24–36 hours until almost completely dry but still a bit pliable.

"SOUR CREAM" Blend all ingredients in a Vita-Mix until completely smooth. Refrigerate until firm.

TOMATO Toss all ingredients together and season to taste.

ASSEMBLY Spread a thin layer of "sour cream" on each piece of bruschetta and top with a generous amount of tomatoes. Garnish with basil and black pepper. SERVES 4–6

orange, pistachio-cacao, and mesquite truffles

When I first began experimenting with raw food, my need for snacking was more present than it is today—but I still keep truffles, chocolate, or some sweet treat in my home. Raw truffles are easy to make and keep well when refrigerated or even frozen. These three are some of my favorite variations. The mesquite gives them a very smoky earth flavor, and the others are more traditional. Any variation of citrus and nuts will always be perfectly workable.

TRUFFLE BASE
3 cups cacao powder
4 cups soaked cashews
4 cups tahini
2 cups coconut oil
3 teaspoons vanilla extract
1 teaspoon sea salt
4 cups raw agave
3 teaspoons cinnamon
1 teaspoon nutmeg

ORANGE POWDER
1 cup chopped orange zest

PISTACHIO-CACAO CENTER
1 cup pistachios, soaked 4–5 hours
$1/2$ cup cacao nibs
$1/4$ cup raw agave
3 tablespoons coconut butter
$1/4$ teaspoon salt

MESQUITE-MACA-MAPLE SUGAR
$1/4$ cup mesquite powder
$1/4$ cup maca powder
$1/3$ cup maple sugar

TRUFFLE BASE Blend all ingredients in a Vita-Mix. Separate into thirds and freeze until firm and not sticky.

ORANGE POWDER Dehydrate 24–36 hours. Pulverize in a coffee grinder, mortar, or small food processor.

PISTACHIO-CACAO CENTER Pulse all ingredients in a food processor until combined. Roll into balls smaller than a marble; freeze on wax paper.

MESQUITE-MACA-MAPLE SUGAR Combine all ingredients.

ASSEMBLY FOR THE ORANGE Scoop out 1 tablespoon of truffle and roll into a ball. Roll in orange powder and freeze until ready to serve.

ASSEMBLY FOR THE PISTACHIO-CACAO This will take a little practice. Using a tablespoon, scoop out a spoonful of truffle base and wrap around pistachio center. Roll into balls and freeze until just before serving.

ASSEMBLY FOR THE MESQUITE Scoop out 1 tablespoon of truffle and roll into a ball. Roll in mesquite sugar and freeze until ready to serve. YIELDS 75–80 TRUFFLES

picadillo santiaguero, arroz amarillo, y mariquitas: portobello-meat stew with yellow "rice," crisp plantain, and macadamia "sour cream"

Picadillo is a stew-like dish served in Latin America, traditionally with beef. This version uses the meaty portobello mushroom instead. The Cuban version of this dish has olives, as does this recipe. It can be eaten on its own with "rice" but the mixture can also be eaten in a taco shell.

PICADILLO
4 cups chopped portobello mushrooms
1/4 cup green or black olives, pitted and chopped
Olive oil
Salt
Black pepper
2 tablespoons sun-dried tomatoes, soaked, drained, and chopped
1/4 cup raisins, soaked
1/4 cup chopped green bell pepper
Pinch sea salt

YELLOW "RICE"
4 cups chopped jicama
1 cup coconut meat
6 tablespoons carrot juice
1 tablespoon raw agave
1 tablespoon fresh lime juice

1/2 teaspoon turmeric
Pinch salt
Pinch cayenne

PLANTAIN
1 plantain
Coconut oil to brush
Salt

"SOUR CREAM"
1 cup macadamia nuts, soaked 1–2 hours
1/2 cup water
1/4 cup olive oil
4 1/2 teaspoons fresh lemon juice
3/4 teaspoon salt

GARNISH
1/2 cup "sour cream" (see above)
Cilantro sprigs

PICADILLO Toss portobello mushrooms and green peppers in olive oil. Place on Teflex sheets and dehydrate 45–60 minutes. Combine remaining ingredients and mix well. Dehydrate together another 30 minutes and reserve.

YELLOW "RICE" Pulse-chop jicama in a food processor until ricelike consistency is achieved. Blend remaining ingredients in a Vita-Mix until very smooth. Mix with yellow "rice." Set aside.

PLANTAIN Slice plantain on a diagonal into thin slices. Brush with coconut oil and sprinkle with salt. Place on dehydrator screens and dehydrate until crisp.

"SOUR CREAM" Blend all ingredients in Vita-Mix until completely smooth. Store in refrigerator.

ASSEMBLY Place a ring mold in the center of a plate. Fill with 1/4 cup yellow "rice" and press. Put 1/4 cup picadillo on top and gently press. Carefully remove the ring mold. Stick in 5 plantain chips. Using a squeeze bottle, drizzle with "sour cream" and garnish with cilantro sprigs. Repeat for remaining 3 servings. **SERVES 4**

natilla de chocolate, majarete y turron de coco: chocolate pudding, sweet corn flan, coffee-cinnamon syrup, and crispy chile macaroons

If every dessert were simply chocolate or fruit, life in the kitchen might not be that entertaining. Whenever possible, we like to incorporate vegetables or herbs into a dessert in a subtle way as a means to offer our guests a challenging flavor, something new, and a dessert that they will remember us by—hopefully in a fond way.

PUDDING
3/4 cup cashews, soaked 1–2 hours
3/4 cup coconut meat
6 tablespoons water
1/2 cup raw agave
6 tablespoons melted coconut oil
1/2 teaspoon vanilla extract
1/4 teaspoon sea salt
1/2 cup cocoa powder
3/4 teaspoon raw carob powder

FLAN
3/4 cup fresh yellow corn
3/4 cup cashews, soaked
1/2 cup coconut meat
1/2 teaspoon vanilla extract
1/4 teaspoon salt
1/4 cup raw agave
6 tablespoons coconut oil
6 tablespoons coconut flour
1/2 teaspoon cinnamon

MACAROONS
1 cup coconut flakes, ground to powder
1 cup cashew flour
1/2 cup flax meal
3/4 teaspoon cinnamon
1 teaspoon ancho chile powder
Pinch salt
6 tablespoons maple syrup
2 tablespoons coconut oil, melted
3/4 teaspoon vanilla extract

SYRUP
1/2 cup raw agave
1 teaspoon cinnamon
1/2 teaspoon coffee extract
1/4 vanilla bean, scraped
Pinch salt

GARNISH
1/4 cup fresh corn
Mint sprigs

PUDDING Blend all ingredients in a Vita-Mix until completely smooth. Place in refrigerator for 5–6 hours or freeze for 1–2 hours prior to serving.

FLAN Blend all ingredients until smooth in Vita-Mix. Pour into small ramekins; refrigerate 5–6 hours or freeze 1–2 hours prior to serving.

MACAROONS Mix together dry ingredients. Add wet ingredients to dry mixture and mix thoroughly. Spread 1/2 inch thick onto dehydrator Teflex sheets. Dehydrate 24–48 hours. Cut into desired shapes and transfer to dehydrator screens; dehydrate another 8–10 hours.

SYRUP Blend ingredients until smooth in Vita-Mix.

ASSEMBLY Place 1 scoop flan and a quenelle of pudding on each plate. Arrange with macaroons and corn; garnish with mint and drizzle with syrup. SERVES 4–6

chile rellenos, monta-raw jack "cheese," and cacao mole

This dish was first prepared by Kristen Reyes and Justin Baumgartner for a Mexican dinner I was hosting. When I first saw it, I could not believe the colors—bright green pepper offset by an orange cheese, golden corn filling, and chocolate mole—and it tastes every bit as complex and satisfying as it appears. I would venture to say that, strictly as a consumer, this would be my favorite dish to enjoy with a good glass of wine.

RELLENOS FILLING
2 cups fresh corn
2 cups sliced and quartered zucchini
1 cup diced red bell pepper
1 cup diced tomato
3/4 cup minced red onion
1 tablespoon minced jalapeño
1 tablespoon chopped fresh cilantro
1 tablespoon fresh lime juice
1/4 teaspoon cumin
Pinch cayenne
Pinch chili powder
Salt and black pepper to taste

"CHEESE"
3 1/2 cups macadamia nuts, soaked 1–2 hours
3/4 cup olive oil
1/4 shallot, diced
1 clove garlic
2 tablespoons fresh lemon juice
1 tablespoon sea salt
3 tablespoons nutritional yeast
3/4 teaspoon chili powder
Pinch cayenne

CACAO MOLE
2 dried ancho or chipotle chiles, soaked 2–3 hours
1/4 cup chopped red onion
1 clove garlic
1 tablespoon sunflower seeds, soaked 4–6 hours
1/4 cup almond butter
1/4 cup raisins, soaked 20–30 minutes
3 tablespoons olive oil
1/2 cup water
2 tablespoons raw agave
1/2 cup cacao powder
1 teaspoon ground cumin
1/4 teaspoon ground coriander
1/2 teaspoon salt
Pinch cayenne
Black pepper to taste

RED PEPPER SAUCE
2 cups chopped red bell peppers
1 red chile pepper, seeded and minced
1/2 cup cashews, soaked 2 hours
1/4 cup water
1 tablespoon fresh lime juice
2 tablespoons raw agave
Salt to taste

GARNISH
4–6 fresh poblano or Anaheim chiles or red lipstick peppers

RELLENOS FILLING Combine all ingredients in a bowl and let sit 15–20 minutes prior to using.

"CHEESE" Place all ingredients in a food processor. Allow to process up to 5 minutes; scrape sides of processor with a spatula to be sure all ingredients are completely combined.

CACAO MOLE Blend all ingredients in a Vita-Mix until smooth.

RED PEPPER SAUCE Blend all ingredients in Vita-Mix until smooth.

ASSEMBLY Cut the chiles or peppers in half and stuff each with equal amounts of "cheese" and rellenos filling. Place stuffed chiles on a sheet pan, cover with plastic wrap, and dehydrate 2–3 hours. Serve warm with cacao mole and red pepper sauce. SERVES 4–6

tacos de tomates al sol con crema cítric:
tomato tacos with citrus cream

These are flavors that anyone would love and be comfortable with. While I push the boundaries with most of my cuisine, I am also aware of the necessity to provide identifiable foods and have to remind myself that something that may appear simple and familiar may not always be. This recipe is straightforward, for sure, but not like any taco you've ever had.

TACO SHELLS
3/4 cup flax meal
3 cups fresh corn
1 1/2 cups chopped red bell pepper
1 cup water
1/2 small red onion
3/4 clove garlic
1 tablespoon fresh lime juice
1 1/2 teaspoons sea salt
2 teaspoons cumin
Pinch cayenne

CREAM
1 3/4 cups cashews, soaked 1–2 hours
1/2 cup coconut meat

3/4 cup water
6 tablespoons fresh lemon juice
Zest of 4 lemons

TOMATOES
2 cups sun-dried tomatoes, soaked 30–45 minutes
4 chipotle chiles, soaked 1 hour (reserve soaking water)
Salt to taste

SPINACH
4 cups torn spinach
Olive oil to coat
Salt and pepper

GARNISH
Cilantro sprigs for garnish

TACO SHELLS Set flax meal aside. Blend remaining ingredients in a Vita-Mix until smooth. Stir in flax meal. Spread on Teflex sheets in 6-inch circles and dehydrate until able to flip. When tortillas are ready to flip (after 4–6 hours), flip into hard-shell taco shapes using a cylinder to hold taco shell open. Dehydrate another 24 hours.

CREAM Blend all ingredients in Vita-Mix until smooth and creamy. Store in the refrigerator until firm.

TOMATOES Place sun-dried tomatoes and chiles in a food processor and add a small amount of soaking water. Add salt as needed. Pulse-chop until chunky.

SPINACH Toss spinach with remaining ingredients. Place in a bowl and cover with plastic wrap; let sit 15–20 minutes until wilted.

ASSEMBLY Holding the taco shell in 1 hand, fill it with tomatoes, then marinated spinach, and top with Citrus Cream. Place on the plate and garnish with cilantro sprigs.
SERVES 4–6

chocolate ancho chile tarts with lime-spiced mango chutney and cinnamon vanilla cream

I love chocolate and spice or chocolate and salt—perhaps that is why mole is one of my favorite things to eat and the reason I always keep a Jacques Torres "Wicked Chocolate" bar in my kitchen. In this dish, the unexpected spice kick is nicely offset by the cooling quality of the crème anglaise.

TART CRUST
Coconut oil
2 cups Cookie Crumb Flour (see below)

COOKIE CRUMB FLOUR
4 cups cocoa powder
4 cups oat flour
1 cup maple syrup
1 cup agave
3 tablespoons coconut oil, melted
1^1/$_2$ teaspoons Himalayan salt
1^1/$_2$ teaspoons vanilla extract

TART FILLING
1^1/$_2$ cups cashews, soaked
^{1}/$_2$ cup plus 2 tablespoons water
^{1}/$_2$ cup plus 2 tablespoons raw agave
^{1}/$_2$ cup melted coconut oil
^{1}/$_2$ teaspoon vanilla extract
^{1}/$_4$ teaspoon sea salt
^{1}/$_2$ cup plus 2 tablespoons cocoa powder
2 tablespoons ancho chile powder

CHUTNEY, OPTIONAL
1 quart frozen mango, chopped
^{1}/$_2$ cup raw agave
^{1}/$_2$ cup fresh lime juice
^{1}/$_4$ teaspoon ancho chile powder plus more to taste
Pinch cayenne plus more to taste
2 tablespoons lime zest plus more to taste

VANILLA CREAM
^{1}/$_2$ cup cashews, soaked 1–2 hours
^{1}/$_4$ cup coconut meat
^{1}/$_4$ cup raw agave
^{3}/$_4$ cup water
1 teaspoon vanilla extract
^{1}/$_4$ cup coconut oil
^{1}/$_2$ teaspoon cinnamon
Pinch cayenne
Pinch sea salt

TART CRUST Mix enough coconut oil into the cookie flour until it holds together. Press very thin into tart shells and chill in freezer before filling.

COOKIE CRUMB FLOUR Mix dry ingredients thoroughly. Add remaining ingredients to dry ingredients. Mix well with hands. Crumble into small pieces (no bigger than 1/2 inch) onto dehydrator screens. Dehydrate 3 days. Process in a food processor until it reaches a small crumb consistency. Sift to separate crumbs from flour. Crumbs should be no larger than 1/4 inch. Store crumbs and flour in separate containers in refrigerator.

TART FILLING Blend all ingredients in a Vita-Mix until very smooth. Fill cookie crusts and chill in freezer overnight. Re-move tarts from metal shells and wrap in plastic wrap. Store in freezer.

CHUTNEY Place all ingredients in a quart container, then put in a dehydrator at 115 degrees F for 3–4 hours. When mango is thawed and warm, strain and toss with a bit more ancho chile powder, cayenne, and lime zest. Pulse-chop in a food processor to create a very chunky compote.

VANILLA CREAM Blend all ingredients in Vita-Mix until very smooth. Refrigerate until ready to serve.

ASSEMBLY Pour a generous pool of cream on plates, place a tart on top and spoon optional chutney on tarts. **SERVES 4**

oyster mushroom seviche
and bitter orange–lime sauce

The chewy oyster mushrooms are treated in the same way that a traditional recipe would call for marinating fish or shellfish—"cooking" with the acidic component in citrus while absorbing the flavors it sits with. I love marinated oyster mushrooms and find their flavor more pleasant than raw shiitake, which sometimes have a musty taste I don't care for.

SEVICHE
1/4 cup finely chopped red onion
1/2 cup peeled, seeded, and diced fresh plum tomatoes
1/2 medium habanero chile, seeds and ribs removed, chopped into tiny pieces
3/4 cup fresh-squeezed orange juice, strained

1/4 cup fresh-squeezed lime juice, strained
Pinch salt
2 cups oyster mushrooms, torn into thirds lengthwise
1 large avocado, peeled and cut into medium-size dice
4 orange wedges for garnish
4 lime wedges for garnish
Chopped cilantro leaves

SEVICHE In a bowl, mix the onion, tomatoes, habanero, orange juice, lime juice, and salt. Add the oyster mushrooms and mix. Cover very tightly with plastic wrap and refrigerate 2 hours. Add the avocado and mix carefully so it doesn't fall apart. Serve in medium-size martini glasses garnished with an orange wedge, lime wedge, and chopped cilantro.
SERVES 4

summer rolls and
red chili–pineapple dipping sauce

When entertaining, it is always most practical to make use of foods that are easily handled and not in danger of becoming wet or sticky. Dipping sauces are very useful, as they allow guests to apply them only when they are ready to taste, and it creates an interactive experience that adds to the pleasure of eating. I first fell in love with summer rolls at a French Vietnamese restaurant, Le Colonial, in New York. Although summer rolls are traditionally made with rice paper, I actually prefer the use of collard greens, which add flavor.

SUMMER ROLLS
8 collard leaves, cut in half with ribs removed
2 cups julienned carrots, in 3-inch lengths
2 cups julienned cucumbers, in 3-inch lengths
2 medium zucchini, julienned in 3-inch lengths
2 cups julienned young coconut, mango, or papaya
2 red or yellow bell peppers, julienned
2 tablespoons black sesame seeds

DRESSING
1 cup almond butter
2 Roma tomatoes
$1/4$ cup nama shoyu
2 tablespoons sesame oil
2 tablespoons fresh lime juice

2 tablespoons maple syrup
1 teaspoon miso
1 ($1^1/2$-inch) piece ginger
1 ($1/2$-inch) piece lemongrass
3–4 Thai chiles
$1/2$ teaspoon salt

DIPPING SAUCE
2 cups fresh pineapple juice
$1/4$ cup raw agave
1 tablespoon lime juice
1 teaspoon red pepper flakes
$1/2$ teaspoon paprika

ASSEMBLY
$1/2$ cup chopped macadamia nuts

DRESSING Blend all ingredients in a Vita-Mix until completely smooth, adding water as necessary to create a very thick dressing.

DIPPING SAUCE Combine all ingredients in a bowl. Place bowl in dehydrator to reduce overnight.

ASSEMBLY Mix macadamia nuts with enough dressing to hold them together. Place mixture on a collard green wrapper; top with a few of each filling ingredient and black sesame seeds. Roll tightly. If needed, use dressing to hold ends together. Serve with dipping sauce. **SERVES 4–6**

ensalada criolla, cebollas fritas y vinagreta cubana: cuban salad with breaded onion rings and cilantro lime vinaigrette

A Cuban dinner I once hosted was very well received. Most chefs, including myself, have had very little contact with any real Cuban cuisine, yet we have a romanticized vision of it—at least enough to prepare interesting food that connects with the country's passion for artistic expression.

VINAIGRETTE
1/2 cup olive oil
1/4 cup fresh lime juice
1/2 clove garlic
1/4 cup fresh cilantro
2 tablespoons fresh parsley
Pinch salt

ONION RINGS
1 medium red onion, sliced into 1/4-inch-thick rings
1 cup olive oil
1 cup almond flour
1/4 cup oat flour
1/2 teaspoon sea salt

1/4 cup flax meal
1 1/2 teaspoons nutritional yeast
1/4 teaspoon dried oregano

RED BELL PEPPER DUST
4 medium red bell peppers, roughly chopped

ASSEMBLY
8 cups roughly chopped romaine lettuce
1 cup quartered red cherry tomatoes
3/4 cup lime vinaigrette (see upper left)
1 cup diced pineapple
1 ripe avocado, peeled, pitted, and sliced
12 breaded onion rings (see left)
Fresh cilantro sprigs
Red bell pepper dust (see above)

VINAIGRETTE Blend olive oil, lime juice, and garlic in a Vita-Mix until smooth. Add cilantro and parsley, and blend until well combined but not completely smooth. Season with salt.

ONION RINGS Separate onion rings and place in a bowl of ice-cold water for 30 minutes; drain and pat dry with a paper towel. Place olive oil in a small bowl; set aside. Mix remaining ingredients in a medium-size bowl to make crumb mixture. Place 1/4 cup crumb mixture in a small bowl. Dip onion rings, one at a time, into olive oil, then place into the small bowl of the crumb mixture and coat well. Place on dehydrator screens and dehydrate 24–48 hours at 118 degrees F.

RED BELL PEPPER DUST Place red bell peppers on dehydrator screens for 24–48 hours until very dry. Blend in Vita-Mix until reduced to powder. Store in containers in your spice rack.

ASSEMBLY Place the romaine, tomatoes, and 1/2 cup of the vinaigrette in a medium-size bowl; toss until well combined. Divide salad mixture between 4 serving plates; sprinkle each salad with the pineapple, then top with avocado slices, and drizzle with a bit of remaining vinaigrette. Top each salad with 3–4 onion rings, a few fresh cilantro sprigs, and a sprinkle of red bell pepper dust. SERVES 4

mediterranean mini tartlets

Hors d'oeuvres have evolved tremendously over the past ten years; when I was first in New York, working at Christie's auction house, some of the most elaborate parties I have ever seen were directed by large, upscale catering companies. I vividly remember the fun I had tasting all of their beautiful creations. Still, very few were vegetarian. There would be cheese tarts, or foie gras pâté, but nothing like these little bites of fresh vegetables and their nutty crusts. Most of our small dishes can be made successfully in larger portions as well.

CRUST
2 cups almonds, processed to crumb form
1/2 cup cashew flour
1/2 tablespoon salt
1 tablespoon nutritional yeast
3 tablespoons olive oil
1/4 cup water
1/2 tablespoon cumin

HUMMUS
1 cup cashews, soaked 1–2 hours
1/2 cup macadamia nuts, soaked 1–2 hours
3 tablespoons fresh lemon juice
1 1/2 tablespoons olive oil
1/4 cup tahini
3/4 teaspoon salt
1/2 clove garlic
1/2–2/3 cup water

TOMATOES
2 cups halved or thinly sliced cherry tomatoes
1/4 cup olive oil
Salt and pepper to taste

TAPENADE
1/4 cup olive oil
1 1/2 cups pitted green olives
1 tablespoon lemon juice
1 tablespoon chopped parsley
Black pepper to taste

GARNISH
1/2 cup diced cucumber
3 tablespoons chopped parsley

CRUST Mix all ingredients in a bowl with hands. Press into plastic-lined mini tart shells and dehydrate 4–5 hours. Remove from plastic and place on dehydrator screens; dehydrate overnight.

HUMMUS Blend all ingredients in a Vita-Mix until completely smooth, adding water only as necessary to form a thick purée. Pour into a piping bag.

TOMATOES Toss cherry tomatoes with olive oil, salt, and pepper. Spread on Teflex sheets and dehydrate 20–30 minutes.

TAPENADE Blend ingredients in a Vita-Mix until smooth.

ASSEMBLY Stir cucumber into hummus. Fill tart shells with hummus and top with marinated tomatoes. Drizzle with tapenade and finish with chopped parsley. YIELDS 2 DOZEN

tricolor sesame-cashew dumplings and sweet chile–lime sauce

These beautiful dumplings appear like flowers on a large tray. They were originally an idea put together for a large party I catered in the summer for seven hundred people. The only problem with these dumplings is that they will disappear before a server can get more than five feet past the kitchen—guests devour them by the handful!

WRAPPERS
3 cups chopped coconut meat, divided
$1/2$ teaspoon sea salt, divided
$1/4$ cup each beet, carrot, and spinach juice

FILLING
4 cups cashews, soaked 1–2 hours
$1/4$ cup nama shoyu
$1/4$ cup sesame oil
$1/4$ cup raw tahini
1 tablespoon lime juice
2 tablespoons chopped fresh ginger

SAUCE
$1/2$ cup nama shoyu
2 tablespoons raw agave

2 tablespoons fresh lime juice
1 tablespoon sesame oil
Pinch dried chile flakes

ASSEMBLY
3 cups torn spinach
$1^1/2$ teaspoons sesame oil
$3/4$ teaspoon finely diced fresh ginger
Pinch sea salt
$1/4$ teaspoon chili powder
$1/2$ teaspoon sesame seeds
2 cups Sesame-Cashew Filling (see left)
1 cup finely diced carrot
$1/2$ cup finely diced scallions
1 cup finely diced celery
Chives

WRAPPERS Blend 1 cup coconut meat, a pinch salt, and beet juice in a Vita-Mix until very smooth. Spread mixture in a thin even layer over a Teflex sheet and dehydrate 3 hours. Repeat process separately with carrot and spinach juices. Trim edges and cut into 9 squares. Store in plastic wrap in the refrigerator until ready to use. Remove wrappers from refrigerator and allow them to come to room temperature prior to use.

FILLING Process all ingredients in a food processor to a chunky consistency.

SAUCE Combine all ingredients in a medium-size bowl and whisk until well combined.

ASSEMBLY Toss the spinach with the sesame oil, ginger, salt, chili powder, and sesame seeds. Allow to marinate 1 hour; or spread on Teflex sheet, cover with plastic wrap, and place in a dehydrator at 118 degrees F for 10–15 minutes. In a bowl, mix filling, carrot, scallions, and celery. Lay out dumpling wrappers on a workspace and place a small amount of spinach on each. Top with 1 tablespoon filling mixture. Pull up edges around filling to form a beggar's purse and tie with a half chive. Serve with sauce. YIELDS 24

empadinhas de queijo: "cheese" empanadas

These are addictively tasty and surprisingly cheeselike. Although these are more like tartlets, their character is derived from empanadas. Try eating only one—and good luck with that!

SHELLS
2 cups pine nuts, soaked 1–2 hours
2 tablespoons nutritional yeast
$1/2$ teaspoon salt
$1/2$ cup water

FILLING
$1/2$ cup coconut meat
$2/3$ cup cashews, soaked 1–2 hours

$1/3$ cup Irish moss
$1/4$ cup water
1 teaspoon sea salt
1 teaspoon nutritional yeast
1 tablespoon fresh lemon juice
1 tablespoon yellow pepper powder, optional
$1/2$ teaspoon dried oregano

SHELLS Pulse nuts in a food processor to break up. Add yeast, salt, and water; blend until smooth. Spread in small plastic-lined tart shells; dehydrate 24 hours.

FILLING Blend all ingredients except dried oregano in a Vita-Mix until completely smooth. Pulse in dried oregano. Pour into tart crusts. **SERVES 4–6**

sushi and nigiri: inside-out elephant roll with chipotle mayo, banana-banana with umeboshi wasabi sauce, and pickled lotus nigiri

Like dumplings, everyone seems to love sushi these days, even when the "rice" is made with jicama and the "mayo" is made from young coconut meat. I have taken liberty with the Japanese cuisine, infusing influences of Thailand and even Latin America. These variations on their own are ample as a quick cocktail starter before a dinner party.

SUSHI "RICE"
6 cups peeled and roughly chopped jicama
1/2 cup pine nuts
2 teaspoons sea salt
3 tablespoons rice wine vinegar
3 tablespoons raw agave

"MAYO"
1/4 cup macadamia nuts, soaked 1–2 hours
1/2 small, dried chipotle chile, soaked 1–2 hours
1/4 cup soaking water from chipotle chile
1/4 cup cold-pressed extra-virgin olive oil
Sea salt to taste

INSIDE-OUT ELEPHANT ROLL
1/2 portobello mushroom, stemmed and sliced about
    1/2 inch thick
1 1/2 teaspoons nama shoyu
1 tablespoon cold-pressed sesame oil
1 sheet untoasted nori
1/2 cup sushi "rice" (see above)
2 tablespoons "mayo" (see above)
1/4 cup torn baby spinach
1/4 red bell pepper, sliced into strips
1 whole scallion
1/2 avocado, peeled

BANANA-BANANA
1 teaspoon umeboshi plum paste
1/2 teaspoon wasabi powder
1 sheet untoasted nori
1/2 cup sushi "rice" (see left)
1/4 medium banana, peeled
2 tablespoons chopped watercress
1 tablespoon fresh cilantro leaves
2 tablespoons peeled and julienned green papaya
10–12 whole enoki mushrooms

NIGIRI
4 small shiitake mushrooms, stems removed
1/2 teaspoon nama shoyu
1 teaspoon cold-pressed sesame oil
1 cup sushi "rice" (see left)
4 thin slices fresh mango, cut into 2 x 1-inch rectangles
Untoasted nori sheet (optional)

PICKLED GINGER
2 tablespoons peeled and finely sliced fresh ginger
1/4 cup raw apple cider vinegar
1 tablespoon raw agave
1 tablespoon beet juice or shredded beet, optional

ASSEMBLY
2 teaspoons wasabi paste
1/2 cup nama shoyu
Pickled ginger

SUSHI "RICE" Process jicama and pine nuts in a food processor until a ricelike consistency is achieved. Do not overprocess! Dry mixture between paper towels or strain through cheesecloth to remove excess moisture. In a medium bowl, whisk together the salt, vinegar, and agave. Add jicama "rice" and toss until well combined. Sprinkle mixture over a dehydrator screen and dehydrate 1–2 hours to remove excess moisture.

"MAYO" Blend all ingredients in a Vita-Mix until very smooth. Store in the refrigerator until ready to use.

INSIDE-OUT ELEPHANT ROLL In a medium bowl, toss portobello mushroom slices with nama shoyu and sesame oil. Spread marinated slices on dehydrator screens and dehydrate 40 minutes, or place in a warm area for 1–2 hours until soft. Lay nori sheet shiny-side down on bamboo mat. Spread sushi "rice" over ¾ of the nori, leaving about 1 inch at the end of the nori sheet uncovered. In the middle of the rice, horizontally spread the "mayo"; then top with spinach, bell pepper, whole scallion, and marinated portobello. Roll sushi tightly. Wet end of nori to ensure it holds securely.

Transfer to a cutting board; cut off the ends with a very sharp or serrated knife, then cut into 8 equal pieces; place 3 slices, standing up, in the corner of each serving plate.

Just before serving, cut the avocado in very thin slices and lay 1–2 slices over each piece of sushi. You may need to trim the avocado to ft the sushi piece perfectly.

BANANA-BANANA In a small bowl, mix the plum paste and wasabi powder until well combined. Lay 1 sheet nori shiny-side down on a bamboo mat. Spread umeboshi-wasabi mixture in a horizontal line over the middle of the nori sheet. Spread sushi "rice" over ¾ of the nori and umeboshi-wasabi, leaving about 2 inches at the end of the nori sheet uncovered. Cut banana in half, then in quarters lengthwise, and place in the middle of sushi rice horizontally. Next to the banana, place watercress, cilantro, papaya, and enoki mushrooms. Roll sushi tightly and wet end of nori to ensure it holds securely. Transfer to a cutting board; cut off the ends with a very sharp or serrated knife, then cut into 8 equal pieces; place 3 pieces in the corner of each serving plate, opposite the Inside-Out Elephant Rolls.

NIGIRI Toss shiitake caps in nama shoyu and sesame oil, and let marinate in a warm place for 10–15 minutes. Place about 2 tablespoons sushi "rice" in the palm of your hand and close your hand into a fist to shape the rice; smooth any ridges with your fingers. The mold should be 2 inches long and 1 inch wide. Continue molding all of the rice until you have 8 molds. Place marinated shiitake caps over 4 of the sushi molds; place in an empty corner on each serving plate. Lay mango slices over 4 of the rice molds; place on the plate next to the nigiri.

(Optional: Cut 8 very thin strips from untoasted nori sheet and place across the middle of each piece of nigiri; tuck the ends under the rice.)

PICKLED GINGER Place all ingredients in a container with a lid. Seal container; shake to combine. Let sit 1–2 hours (can store for up to 1 week).

ASSEMBLY Place a small mound (approximately 1 teaspoon) of pickled ginger in the empty corner of each serving dish. Place 1 teaspoon of the wasabi paste next to the ginger and pour nama shoyu in 2 small bowls to be served with the sushi and nigiri. **SERVES 4–6**

blueberry and sweet "cream cheese" mini tartlet

One of the first desserts a budding young chef will learn at The French Culinary Institute is a Tarte de Fruits, or fruit tart, with traditional egg-based crème anglaise and fresh glazed fruit. I love the technique but find the dessert too sweet and sticky—whereas the raw version is so fresh and every bit as decadent. Perhaps this is a young chef's revolution.

TART CRUSTS
2 cups Nut Flour (see page 50)
2 tablespoons coconut oil
1 tablespoon lemon zest

"CREAM CHEESE"
2^1/$_2$ cups cashews, soaked 1–2 hours
^{1}/$_2$ cup coconut meat
^{1}/$_4$ cup fresh lemon juice
^{3}/$_4$ cup raw agave

^{3}/$_4$ cup coconut oil, melted
^{1}/$_2$ cup water
1 teaspoon vanilla extract
^{1}/$_2$ teaspoon sea salt
1 vanilla bean, scraped

GARNISH
2 cups fresh blueberries
Micro mint sprigs

TART CRUSTS Combine all ingredients and press into lined tart shells.

"CREAM CHEESE" Blend all ingredients in a Vita-Mix until very smooth. Fill tart crusts and chill in the freezer overnight. Remove tarts from metal shells and wrap in plastic wrap. Store on sheet pans in the freezer.

ASSEMBLY Garnish tarts with blueberries and mint sprigs.
YIELDS 2 DOZEN

almond-lavender pie in coconut-macaroon crust

Lavender needs to be used in moderation—overdoing it can create a somewhat uncomfortable flavor—but when properly used, especially in a creamy dessert, it can achieve ethereal results.

CRUST

3 cups shredded coconut
1 cup cashew flour
1/2 teaspoon salt
1/4 cup maple syrup
2 tablespoons coconut oil
2 tablespoons date paste

FILLING

3 cups cashews, soaked 1–2 hours

1/2 cup fresh lemon juice
1/2 cup raw agave
3/4 cup coconut oil, melted
1/2 cup water
1 teaspoon vanilla extract
1/2 teaspoon nutritional yeast
1/2 teaspoon sea salt
1/4 vanilla bean, scraped
2 teaspoons almond extract
2 tablespoons chopped lavender

CRUST Mix all ingredients together well by hand. Press into 12-inch tart shells to desired thickness. (Optional: dehydrate 24–48 hours.) Chill crust in the freezer for at least 15 minutes or until ready to fill.

FILLING Blend all ingredients in a Vita-Mix until very smooth.

ASSEMBLY Place filling in a piping bag and pipe into the mini crusts. Chill in freezer 1–2 hours or place in refrigerator overnight. SERVES 8

meaning and reality were not hidden somewhere behind things, they were in them, in all of them.
—Hermann Hesse

meaningful

It was well into my raw food journey that I realized my personal preferences were mostly aligned with the Sattvic Diet, which is traditionally defined as pure, clean, and wholesome. Individuals have their own needs and tastes, and I understand that my approach may not be best for everyone; but when I learned the history behind it, food as a whole began to make more sense to me. Understanding our relationship with food is a lifelong pursuit, and being a chef can complicate that learning process even more. In addition to our own choices, we are faced with countless historic, family, and social traditions, as well as others that we pick up along the way in our own lives.

While raw food as a whole does not have many long-standing traditions, its influence is firmly connected to many foods of years past, both vegetarian and otherwise. Many people are aware of a connection between spirituality and vegetarianism but are not always aware of the reason for that. Over time, my style of raw food has become influenced by three factors: seasonal ingredients, various forms of art, and history. Food has meaning to everyone throughout the world, and in order for it to be significant, it should share one of the many connections we form in our lives. Because of this, I like to remain focused on the influences behind food and what it means to those who enjoy it, in terms of both their experience and, ultimately, their memory.

A meal can serve as a reminder of nearly anything in life—good fortune, a New Year's celebration, breaking a fast, long life, love, and much more. While I take liberty with how to actually prepare the recipes, they are quite often grounded by their connection to these meanings.

Many of the recipes in this chapter are based on very classic recipes while others are loose interpretations, but all share the same value of respect for tradition and meaning when sharing a meal.

zaru somen and sweet dashi sake broth

Zaru noodles are named for the slatted box they are traditionally served in and are a Japanese New Year's favorite, symbolic of long life. The coconut "noodles" in this recipe are so durable that they are able to carry the intense but light flavors of the broth. The night this was on a menu I prepared, I had three bowls and was full for the night.

BROTH
1 cup water
1 cup nama shoyu
2 tablespoons dried dulse
1 tablespoon dried wakame
1/4 cup brown rice vinegar
2 tablespoons raw agave
1 tablespoon fresh lime juice

SOMEN
2 cups young Thai coconut meat
2 tablespoons black sesame seeds
1 1/2 teaspoons shichimi spice
2 tablespoons finely sliced scallion

BROTH Blend water, nama shoyu, dulse, and wakame in a blender until smooth. Strain through a fine sieve into a medium-size bowl. Whisk in remaining ingredients. Store in refrigerator until ready to serve. When ready to serve, pour 1/4 cup broth in the bottom of two small serving bowls.

SOMEN Slice coconut meat into very thin, uniform noodles. Place equal amounts of coconut noodles in each serving bowl with broth. Top each with a sprinkle of black sesame seeds, shichimi, and scallion. Serve immediately. **SERVES 4**

ba bao fan blessing eight-treasure "rice": candied fruits with "longan" syrup

Eight treasure rice is a Chinese New Year's favorite, prepared to bring in good spirits and fortune. It is a pudding-like dessert typically made with eight types of freshly dried fruits and sometimes lotus seeds. I loved the festive look of this dish, not to mention the great flavor.

SWEET "RICE"
2 cups jicama, chopped
1 cup pine nuts, soaked for one hour
1/2 cup agave nectar
1 tablespoon vanilla
2 tablespoons coconut oil

FRUITS AND NUTS
1/2 cup dried cherries, rehydrated
1/2 cup golden raisins
1/2 cup diced lychee or mango
1/2 cup chopped almonds
1/2 cup chopped pistachios

1/2 cup thinly sliced dried apricots
1 cup agave

"LONGAN" SYRUP
1 cup agave
1 teaspoon minced ginger
1/2 cup diced lychee or mango

ASSEMBLY
1/4 cup coconut oil
1/4 cup very fine julienne of orange zest
1/2 cup dried coconut flakes

SWEET "RICE" Pulse jicama and pine nuts in food processor until they have a ricelike consistency. Squeeze out excess water and dehydrate on Teflex sheets for 1½ hours. Add remaining ingredients.

FRUITS AND NUTS Combine all ingredients.

SYRUP Blend ingredients well in a Vita-Mix.

ASSEMBLY Line small bowl with plastic wrap—lightly oil the wrap with coconut oil. Press fruits and nuts all over the wrap and then "rice" firmly on top. Allow to rest for 10 minutes, invert, and remove plastic wrap. Top with orange zest and coconut flakes. Serve with syrup. **SERVES 4–6**

pearl balls with spicy mango salsa

These traditionally glutinous rice balls are a Chinese favorite for New Year's and other celebrations—they symbolize union and togetherness. I actually prefer a raw version far more as it is much lighter and to me, more flavorful.

> If we should be blessed by some great reward, such as fame or fortune, it's the fruit of a seed planted by us in the past. —*Bodhidharma*

PORTOBELLO "MEATBALLS"
4 portobello mushrooms
$1/2$ cup olive oil
Sea salt to taste
Black pepper to taste
2 tablespoons fresh thyme
$1/4$ cup lemon juice
1 clove garlic
$1/2$ cup walnuts, soaked 8–10 hours

STICKY "RICE"
3 cups diced jicama
$1/4$ cup pine nuts
2 tablespoons brown rice vinegar
2 tablespoons raw agave
1 tablespoon salt

SPICY MANGO SALSA
1 cup diced mango
1 red chile, seeded and diced
2 tablespoons fresh lime juice
2 tablespoons chopped cilantro
Pinch salt
1 tablespoon raw agave
1 tablespoon tamarind paste
Water

ASSEMBLY
$1/4$ cup black sesame seeds
$1/4$ cup finely chopped white sesame seeds
1 head baby bok choy

PORTOBELLO "MEATBALLS" Roughly chop mushrooms and toss in olive oil, salt, pepper, thyme, and lemon juice; spread on Teflex sheets and let dehydrate 45 minutes. Process garlic and walnuts in a food processor until chunky; place in a bowl. Roll mixture into $3/4$-inch "meatballs" and dehydrate until firm on the outside and moist on the inside.

STICKY "RICE" Process jicama and pine nuts until they are finely minced, similar in size to rice grains. Dry with towels to remove excess liquid. Combine "rice" with vinegar, agave and salt. Spread mixture onto dehydrator screens and dehydrate 90 minutes, fluffing occasionally.

SPICY MANGO SALSA Blend all ingredients in a Vita-Mix. Add water if needed to thin.

ASSEMBLY Cover portobello "meatballs" with a thin layer of sticky "rice" by hand, squeezing to form a circular shape. Roll in black and white sesame seeds. To serve, play Pearl Balls on bok choy leaves and serve with dipping sauce on the side. SERVES 4

mochi "ice cream": goji berry, vanilla lemongrass, green tea

Mochi means "rice cake," and they are another traditional New Year's food, due to their resemblance of the mirror decorating the Shinto Shrine. They are a traditional Japanese food at holidays and festivals, including January 11, which is called "Mirror Opening Day." The origin of the name has three translated meanings, including "full moon," "from God," and "stickiness."

MOCHI
1 cup cashews, soaked 1–2 hours
3/4 cup young Thai coconut meat
1/4 cup raw agave
1/4 cup raw coconut oil
Pinch sea salt
1/4 teaspoon nonalcohol vanilla extract
Few drops nonalcohol almond extract
1/2 cup oat flour*
3/4 cup coconut flour**

GOJI BERRY "ICE CREAM"
1/2 cup cashews, soaked 1–2 hours
1/2 cup macadamia nuts, soaked 1–2 hours
1/2 cup young Thai coconut meat
3/4 cup raw agave nectar
1 1/2 cups water
2 teaspoons nonalcohol vanilla extract

1 teaspoon fresh lemon juice
Pinch sea salt
1/2 cup coconut oil
1 cup soaked goji berries, blended and strained
    through a fine sieve

VANILLA LEMONGRASS "ICE CREAM"
1/2 cup cashews, soaked 1–2 hours
1/2 cup macadamia nuts, soaked 1–2 hours
1/2 cup young Thai coconut meat
3/4 cup raw agave nectar
1 1/2 cups water
2 teaspoons nonalcohol vanilla extract
1/4 vanilla bean, scraped
1/4 cup lemongrass juice
Pinch sea salt
1/2 cup coconut oil

MOCHI Blend first 7 ingredients in a Vita-Mix until very smooth and creamy. Transfer mixture to a medium-size bowl and stir in flours until it is very well combined and lumps are smoothed out. Line a 9 x 13-inch pan with plastic wrap on bottom and sides. Pour dough into prepared pan and spread very thin, approximately 1/2 inch thick. Place in freezer until firm.

*NOTE: Oat flour is made by grinding whole raw oat groats in a high-speed blender or a coffee or spice grinder, until a very fine flour is achieved.

**NOTE: Coconut flour is made by grinding dried coconut flakes in a high-speed blender or a coffee or spice grinder, until a fine flour is achieved. Do not overprocess or the oils in the coconut will cause the coconut to cake.

GOJI BERRY "ICE CREAM" Blend all ingredients in Vita-Mix until very smooth. Pour into an ice cream maker and follow manufacturer's instructions; or freeze base in a square pan, cut, and run through a masticating juicer (such as the Champion or Greenstar). Freeze overnight. Scoop 2 large rounded scoops of "ice cream" into a pan or plate; freeze until very firm.

VANILLA LEMONGRASS "ICE CREAM" Blend all ingredients in Vita-Mix until very smooth. Pour into ice cream maker and follow manufacturer's instructions; or freeze base in square pan, cut, and run through masticating juicer (such as the Champion or Greenstar). Freeze overnight. Scoop 2 large rounded scoops of "ice cream" into pan or plate; freeze until very firm.

continued on page 220

GREEN TEA "ICE CREAM"
1/2 cup cashews, soaked 1–2 hours
1/2 cup macadamia nuts, soaked 1–2 hours
1/2 cup young Thai coconut meat
1/2 cup raw agave
11/2 cups water
2 teaspoons nonalcohol vanilla extract
21/2 tablespoons green tea powder
Pinch sea salt
1/2 cup coconut oil

BLACK CACAO SYRUP
11/2 cups raw agave
1/2 cup raw cacao powder
2 tablespoons raw carob powder
1/4 teaspoon nonalcohol vanilla extract
Pinch sea salt
1/2 cup coconut oil

ASSEMBLY
Oat flour
Mint or basil sprigs

GREEN TEA "ICE CREAM" Blend all ingredients in Vita-Mix until very smooth. Pour into ice cream maker and follow manufacturer's instructions; or freeze base in square pan, cut, and run through masticating juicer (such as the Champion or Greenstar). Freeze overnight. Scoop 2 large rounded scoops of ice cream into pan or plate; freeze until very firm.

BLACK CACAO SYRUP Blend all ingredients in a blender until smooth. Keep in a warm area until ready to serve.

ASSEMBLY Dust a dry cutting board with oat flour. Turn out frozen mochi onto cutting board and peel off plastic. Cut six 4 x 4-inch pieces. With floured hands, flatten each piece until very thin. Place 1 scoop of ice cream in the center of each mochi sheet and mold mochi around ice cream until ice cream is completely covered; smooth ridges with fingers.

Place mochi-covered ice cream in freezer immediately and freeze 8–10 hours until completely frozen. To serve, slice ends off each mochi ice cream ball and cut into 2 uniform pieces. Place a slice of each flavor on serving plates and garnish with mint or basil sprigs and cacao syrup. **SERVES 4**

jiaozi three ways: sweet-and-sour tofu with spiced cashews, caramelized shiitake with bamboo shoots, and bok choy with lotus root

Jiaozi is an important part of Chinese culture today, no doubt in part because they are delicious and fun to eat. Everyone loves dumplings. They always appear during spring festivals, generally prepared before midnight on the last day of the lunar year and enjoyed on the first day of the New Year. These are made to look like gold and silver ingots—the Chinese hope that they will bring good fortune and, when sweetened, a sweeter life.

TOFU WITH CASHEWS

WRAPPERS
2 cups chopped coconut meat
3 tablespoons golden beet juice
1/4 teaspoon sea salt

FILLING
2 cups cashews, soaked 1–2 hours
3 tablespoons nama shoyu
3 tablespoons sesame oil
2 tablespoons raw tahini
1 tablespoon chopped fresh ginger

SAUCE (YIELDS 1 CUP)
1/2 cup nama shoyu
2 tablespoons raw agave
2 tablespoons fresh lime juice
1 tablespoon sesame oil
Pinch dried chile flakes

ASSEMBLY
3 cups torn spinach
1 1/2 teaspoons sesame oil
1/2 teaspoon sesame seeds
3/4 teaspoon finely diced fresh ginger
Pinch sea salt
1/4 teaspoon chili powder
2 cups minced cashews, soaked 2–3 hours
1 cup finely diced carrot
1/2 cup finely diced scallions
1 cup finely diced celery

TOFU WITH CASHEWS WRAPPERS Blend all ingredients in a Vita-Mix until very smooth. Spread mixture in a thin even layer over a Teflex sheet and dehydrate 3 hours. Trim edges and cut into 9 squares. Store in plastic wrap in the refrigerator until ready to use. Remove wrappers from refrigerator and allow to come to room temperature prior to use.

TOFU WITH CASHEWS FILLING Process all ingredients in a food processor until chunky consistency is achieved.

TOFU WITH CASHEWS SAUCE Combine all ingredients in a medium-size bowl and whisk until well combined.

ASSEMBLY Toss the spinach with the sesame oil, sesame seeds, ginger, salt, and chili powder. Allow to marinate 1 hour; or spread on a Teflex sheet, cover with plastic wrap, and place in dehydrator at 118 degrees F for 10–15 minutes.

In a bowl, mix cashews, carrot, scallions, and celery. Lay out coconut wrappers on workspace and place a small amount of marinated spinach on top of each. Top with 1 tablespoon of the cashew mixture. Pull up edges around filling to form a half-circle dumpling. Serve with sauce.

continued on page 223

SHIITAKE WITH BAMBOO SHOOTS

WRAPPERS
(see page 221, replace golden beet juice with spinach
juice)

FILLING
1 cup sliced shiitake mushrooms
2 tablespoons sesame oil
1/4 cup finely chopped bamboo shoots
1 tablespoon minced ginger
1/2 cup cashews, soaked 2–3 hours
1 teaspoon minced scallions
1/4 teaspoon minced green chile

MUSTARD SAUCE
1/4 cup white miso
1 tablespoon pulverized mustard seeds
2 tablespoons fresh lemon juice
1/4 cup grapeseed oil
Water to thin

ASSEMBLY
(See page 221)

BOK CHOY WITH LOTUS ROOT

WRAPPERS
(see page 221, replace golden beet juice with carrot
juice)

FILLING
1 small head bok choy, roughly chopped
1/4 cup thinly shaved lotus root
1 tablespoon soy sauce
1 tablespoon sesame oil
1 teaspoon sesame seeds
Salt to taste

GINGER DRESSING
3 tablespoons minced ginger
2 tablespoons fresh lime juice
1 teaspoon raw agave
1/2 teaspoon minced jalapeño
3 tablespoons olive oil
Salt to taste

ASSEMBLY
(See page 221)

FINAL ASSEMBLY
1 bunch chives, cut into 1-inch batons

SHIITAKE WITH BAMBOO SHOOTS FILLING Toss the mushrooms with sesame oil and dehydrate for 2 hours. Combine with remaining ingredients in a food processor just until combined.

MUSTARD SAUCE Blend all ingredients well in a Vita-Mix.

BOK CHOY WITH LOTUS ROOT FILLING Combine all ingredients and dehydrate 1 hour. Finely chop by hand.

GINGER DRESSING Blend all ingredients well in a Vita-Mix.

FINAL ASSEMBLY Place a pool of each of the three sauces on plates. Top with their respective jiaozi. Garnish with chives. SERVES 4–6

cold spicy long-life noodles
with ginger sauce

Chinese noodles symbolize a long life and good health, and therefore should be served very long. Peanuts are actually very rarely available raw, but we were able to find raw peanuts from our friends at rawfood.com that are now available and are excellent in dishes requiring an interesting textural note.

NOODLES
2 large jicama, cut into long noodles with a spiralizer
$^1/_2$ cup roughly chopped wild raw peanuts
$^1/_4$ cup sliced scallions (cut into thin 1-inch slices)
$^1/_2$ cup mung bean sprouts
1 cup roughly chopped bok choy

SAUCE
$^1/_4$ cup sesame oil
$^1/_4$ cup soy sauce
$^1/_4$ cup fresh lemon juice
$^1/_4$ cup tahini
2 tablespoons raw agave
2 tablespoons minced ginger

NOODLES Mix all ingredients by hand.

SAUCE Blend all ingredients well in a Vita-Mix.

ASSEMBLY Toss the noodles with the sauce several times until well coated and serve. **SERVES 4**

vietnamese pho broth with tofu

Pho is the national soup of Vietnam, where it is universally loved. It is also very popular in the United States. There are many theories about its creation—it was invented in the early part of the twentieth century and was influenced by both French and Chinese traditions. Some even claim that its name came from *feu,* derived from the French word for fire, as in *pot-au-feu*, which the French colonialists introduced in Vietnam.

BROTH
1/2 cup nama shoyu
2 tablespoons lemongrass juice
1/4 cup fresh lime juice
1/2 cup olive oil
2 cups celery juice
1/2 cup carrot juice
1/2 cup apple juice
Black pepper
1 teaspoon red pepper flakes
1/2 cup raw agave
1 tablespoon diced red onion
1/2 teaspoon star anise
1 chipotle chile, soaked
1 tablespoon miso
2 tablespoons chopped dulse

TOFU
1 cup cashews, soaked 1–2 hours
1/2 cup fresh young Thai coconut meat
1/2 cup raw carrageenan*
1/4 cup water
1/4 teaspoon sea salt

ASSEMBLY
1/2 cup very fine, long zucchini noodles
1/2 cup very thin coconut noodles
1/4 cup mung bean sprouts
2 tablespoons thinly sliced scallions (sliced on a diagonal)
1/4 cup very thinly sliced red bell pepper
1/4 cup chopped cashews
1 tablespoon black sesame seeds
1/4 cup cilantro leaves

BROTH Blend all ingredients except dulse in a Vita-Mix, then place in a large container. Add dulse and dehydrate 6–8 hours; strain.

TOFU Line the bottom and sides of a small pan or square container with plastic wrap. Drain cashews. Blend all ingredients in a Vita-Mix until completely smooth. Pour into a lined pan (tofu should be about 1 1/2 inches thick) and cover with plastic wrap. Refrigerate about 2 hours until firm. When ready to serve, remove tofu from container by lifting plastic wrap out of pan and gently transferring tofu to a cutting board. Cut into 1/2-inch squares with a butter knife.

*NOTE: Raw carrageenan is prepared by soaking salt-packed Irish moss until all salt is removed. Soak Irish moss overnight, then blend with an equal amount of water until smooth. Store in refrigerator for up to 1 week.

ASSEMBLY Warm pho broth in a dehydrator for 30 minutes. Place half the vegetables in the bottom of soup bowls and top with broth. Pour broth into soup bowls and top with tofu, remaining vegetables, black sesame seeds, and cilantro leaves. SERVES 4

fortune cookies

I added fortune cookies to our Chinese-inspired menu, not fully expecting that my sous chefs Kristen and Anna would be able to actually find a way to make them. Lo and behold, they were perfectly executed. Interestingly, fortune cookies are a California—not a Chinese—invention. They remain a lighthearted and fun way to end the meal, hopefully with a welcoming prophecy.

1¹/₄ cups flax meal
³/₄ cup chopped pear
¹/₂ cup young coconut meat
2 teaspoons lemon juice

¹/₃ cup maple syrup
¹/₂ teaspoon salt
1 teaspoon vanilla
1 cup water

Blend all ingredients in a Vita-mix except water until smooth. Add water until batter is pasty but still thick. Spread into 3-inch circles on Teflex sheets and dehydrate 6–8 hours until firm but still pliable. Place a fortune note on top of each cookie with the end of note barely hanging over the edge. Carefully transer to dehydrator trays and form into fortune cookie shapes, by folding in half, and then folding again to pull down pointed edges. Use paper clips to secure edges if needed. Dehydrate another 18–24 hours until crisp. YIELDS 2 DOZEN

spicy "fried" spring rolls with sweet tamarind fondue

Spring rolls, so named because they are typically eaten during Chinese festivals in the spring, are normally filled with crispy vegetables and sometimes cabbage or mushrooms. They are not always vegetarian, but quite often are. The wrapper in this recipe makes use of one of my favorite techniques and embraces, rather than overpowers, the filling.

WRAPPERS
2 cups flax meal
2 cups chopped yellow squash
1 cup chopped coconut meat
2 tablespoons fresh lemon juice
4 cups water
$1/4$ cup raw agave nectar
1 teaspoon sea salt
1 teaspoon ground coriander
1 teaspoon ground cumin
2 scallions, thinly sliced on a diagonal

FILLING
1 cup julienned carrots
$1/4$ cup sliced scallions
1 cup shredded Napa cabbage
$1^1/2$ cups dried shiitake mushrooms,
    soaked 1 hour and dehydrated 2 hours
$1/2$ teaspoon salt
Black pepper
$1/4$ cup olive oil

TOFU
1 cup cashews, soaked 1–2 hours
$1/2$ cup fresh young Thai coconut meat

$1/2$ cup raw carrageenan (see page 226)
$1/4$ cup water
$1/4$ teaspoon sea salt
$1^1/2$ teaspoons ancho chile powder
$1/4$ teaspoon cayenne
$1/4$ cup cilantro

CHILE SAUCE
$3/4$ teaspoon chipotle chile powder
2 cups cashews, soaked 1–2 hours
$1/4$ teaspoon salt
$1/4$ cup nama shoyu
$1/4$ cup plus 1 tablespoon water

SWEET TAMARIND FONDUE
1 cup dried tamarind paste
$1/2$ cup raw agave
3 tablespoons lime juice
$1/4$ cup coconut water
2 tablespoons water
$1/2$ teaspoon salt

GARNISH
Cilantro leaves

WRAPPERS Blend all ingredients except scallions in a Vita-Mix until smooth; stir in scallions. Spread thinly into 6- to 7-inch rounds on dehydrator Teflex sheets. Dehydrate 5–6 hours until dry but very pliable.

FILLING Fold all ingredients together.

TOFU Line the bottom and sides of a small pan or square container with plastic wrap. Blend all ingredients except cilantro in Vita-Mix until completely smooth; stir in cilantro. Pour into lined pan (tofu should be about 1½ inches thick); cover with plastic wrap. Refrigerate about 2 hours until firm. Remove tofu from container by lifting plastic wrap out of pan and gently transferring to a cutting board. Cut tofu into 2-inch squares with a butter knife.

CHILE SAUCE Blend all ingredients in Vita-Mix until smooth.

SWEET TAMARIND FONDUE Blend all ingredients well in Vita-Mix. Strain through a chinois.

ASSEMBLY Fold the chile sauce into spring roll filling, add tofu, and adjust seasoning. Place a large tablespoon of filling on each spring roll wrapper and spread it out in a row. Fold wrappers tightly. To serve, cut each wrapper on a bias lengthwise, lean one against the other, and garnish with Sweet Tamarind Fondue and cilantro leaves. **SERVES 4**

thai cucumber salad

One of my first experiences with Thai cuisine was during an early chef position I held at a Brazilian restaurant. One evening, I wasn't feeling well and one of the talented cooks, Laisoon Saetio, made a spicy Thai soup with rice. On other occasions, he would prepare cucumber salads with lots of mint and toasted peanuts to go with heartier dishes. In time, the entire kitchen staff would line up for his delicious meals—he and I went on to work together for many years, and this dish is a reminder of his great talent and warm, gentle personality.

SALAD
$1/4$ cup roughly chopped basil
2 medium cucumbers, quartered lengthwise and thinly sliced
1 head butter or Bibb lettuce, torn into small pieces
1 yellow bell pepper, julienned
1 teaspoon salt
$1/4$ cup mint leaves

DRESSING
$3/4$ cup sesame oil
$1/2$ cup nama shoyu

$1/4$ cup olive oil
$1/4$ cup lime juice
1 tablespoon maple syrup
3 Thai chiles or 3 teaspoons red chile flakes
$1/4$ cup cashew butter
Water as needed to thin

GARNISH
$1/3$ cup chopped cashews
2 tablespoons sesame oil
$1/4$ cup diced red pepper

SALAD Combine all salad ingredients in a bowl.

DRESSING Blend all ingredients until smooth in a Vita-Mix.

ASSEMBLY Dress salad generously with dressing and top with cashews, oil, and red pepper. **SERVES 4**

index

NOTE: *Lowercase words denote that it is not the name of a recipe, but that it appears in the recipe.*

A

Agave, Vanilla-, Syrup, 46, **47**
Aleppo Pepper Sauce, 138–40, **139**
Almond/almonds:
  Candied, 118, **119**
  Chutney, Mint-, 128, **129**
  "Gelato," 72, 73
  Lavender Pie in Coconut-Macaroon
    Crust, 207
  Miso-lime-, dressing, 196
  Paste, Marcona, 82, **83**
  Romesco Dumplings, Red Pepper,
    172, **173**
  Tart Shells, 156, **157**
Amaretti, 171
Ancho Chile Tarts, Chocolate, 192, **193**
Anise; *see also* Star Anise
  Syrup, 136, **137**
  Syrup, Chocolate, 96, **97**
Apricot "Yogurt" Cake, 136, **137**
Apricots with Star Anise Syrup and
    Crumble, 42, **43**
Arugula:
  Gnocchi, 152, **153**
  Marinated, 92, **93**
  Pesto, 66, **67**
Asparagus:
  Marinated, 152, **153**
  White, 58, **59**
  White, and Mushrooms with Red
    Pepper Curry Sauce, 68, **69**
  with Bitter Broccoli Ravioli, 90, **91**
Avgolemono, Saffron, 97
Avocado:
  Salsa, 40, **41**
  Tartare, 126, **127**
  Terrine (avocado, beet, mango), 64

B

Ba Bao Fan Blessing Eight-Treasure
    "Rice," 214, **215**
Bacon, Eggplant, 164, **165**
Balsamic Fig Purée, 70, **71**
Bamboo Shoots, Caramelized Shiitake
    with 221–23, **222**

Banana:
  -Banana with Umeboshi Wasabi
    Sauce, 204, **205**
  Ginger Raita, 130, **131**
  "Ice cream," 98
  Lemongrass Cream, 72, **73**
Basil:
  and Spinach-Striped Flan, 62, **63**
  Black Pepper Wrappers, 30, **31**
  "Butter," Frozen, 172, **173**
  "Crème Fraîche," 162, **163**
  "Ice Cream," 50, **51**
  Manti, 148, **149**
  Mousse, 62
  Oil, 38, **39**
  Pistachio Pesto, Mint-, 160, **161**
  Raviolini, 29
  Wafers, Chocolate, 36, **37**
  Wilted Spinach with, 150, **151**
  Wrappers, 82, 83
Beet, mango, and avocado terrine, 64
Beet Ravioli, Spinach and, 150, **151**
Beet Ravioli with Fava Bean Purée and
    Green Herb Oil, 44, **45**
Bitter Orange–Lime Sauce, 194, **195**
Bisteeya, Shiitake, with Ginger-Cilantro
    Sauce, 118, **119**
Blueberry and Sweet "Cream Cheese"
    Mini Tartlet, 206
Bok Choy with Lotus Root, 221–23, **222**
Brazil Nut Truffle Foam, Leek and, 108,
    109
Bread; see also Crackers; Crisp;
    Wrappers
  Cumin Flatbread, 121–22, **121**
  Cornbread Bruschetta, 182
  Garlic and Onion Bread, 164, **165**
  Sumac Flatbread, 138, **139**
  Sun-Dried Tomato Flatbread, 65
Bread crumbs, 107
Brigadeiro, 168, **169**
Brittle, Coconut, 48, **49**
Brittle, Sesame, 124, **125**
Broccoli Rabe, Gnocchi of, with Ginger
    Cream Sauce,76, **77**
Broccoli Rabe, Shiitake Ravioli with, 70, **71**
Broccoli Ravioli, Bitter, 90, **91**
Broth; *see also* Chowder; Soup
  Green Onion, 58, **59**
  Creamy Saffron, 107

Jicama, 164, **165**
Ragout, 28
Sweet Dashi Sake, 212, **213**
Vietnamese Pho Broth with Tofu,
    226, **227**
Bruschetta, Cornbread, 182
"Butter," Frozen Basil, 172, **173**

C

Cacao:
  Crêpes and Sweet Mint Custard with
    Mole, 188, **189**
  Mole, Raw, 88, **89**
  Sauce, Bittersweet, 100, **101**
  Sauce, Black, 98, **99**
  Syrup, Black, 218–20, **219**
  Syrup, Cayenne-, 102, **103**
  Truffles, Pistachio-, 183
Cake:
  Apricot "Yogurt," 136, **137**
  Brigadeiro, 168, **169**
  Chocolate, with Sweet Cherries,
    102, **103**
  Susie Q, with cream filling, 106
Caldo Verde, 164, **165**
Candied:
  Almonds, 118, **119**
  Fruits with "Longan" Syrup, 214, **215**
  Walnuts, 96, **97**
Candy, Mandarin, 78, **79**
Canjica "Ice Cream," 168–70, **169**
Cannelloni, Golden and Green, with
    Sun-Dried Tomato-Ginger Marinara,
    160, **161**
Canneloni, Green Tea, 72, **73**
Cantalope "Gelato," Ginger, 34, **35**
Caramel sauce, 170
Cardamom Foam, White, 62, **63**
Cardamom Kulfi, 134, **135**
Carpaccio, Pineapple, 155
Carpaccio, Plum, 46, **47**
Cashew/Cashews:
  crumble, 42, **43**
  Dumplings, Sesame-, 200, **201**
  "Ricotta," 150, **151**
  Sauce, 221
  Spiced, with Sweet-and-Sour Tofu,
    221–23, **222**
  Wrapper, 221
Caviar, Faded Green, 74, **75**

Caviar, Hijiki, 108
Cayenne-Cacao Syrup, 102, **103**
Chard, Marinated, 164, **165**
"Cheese":
    Crisps, Warm, 80, **81**
    Empanadas, 202, **203**
    Green Tomato–"Ricotta" Tart, 50, **51**
    Macadamia, 30, **31**
    Monta-raw Jack, 188, **189**
    Pignoli "Parmesan" Crisp, 28
    Pine Nut, 90, **91**
Cherries, Chocolate Cake with Sweet, 102, **103**
Cherry Sauce, Raspberry Leaf–Infused, 115
Chile:
    –Lime Sauce, Sweet, 200, **201**
    Macaroons, Crispy, 186, **187**
    Rellenos, 188, **189**
    sauce, 230
    Sauce, Tomato-, 180, **181**
    Tarts, Chocolate, Ancho, 192, **193**
Chili–Pineapple Dipping Sauce, Red, 196, **197**
Chipotle Mayo, 204, 205
Chocolate:
    Cake with Sweet Cherries, 102, **103**
    Fondue, Dark, 94, **95**
    Pudding, 186, **187**
    Pudding, Frozen, 36, **37**
    Sauce, 168
    Sauce, Dark, 48, **49**
    Syrup, Anise, 96, **97**
    Tacos, Chili, 92, **93**
    Tarts, Ancho Chile, 192, **193**
    Wafers, Basil, 36, **37**
    Wrappers, 90, **91**
Chowder; see also Broth; Soup
    Caribbean Conch, 146, **147**
    Yellow Corn, 24, **25**
Chutney:
    Concord Grape, 76, **77**
    Ginger-Tomato, 132, **133**
    Lime-Spiced Mango, 192, **193**
    Mango–Green Papaya, 114
    Mint-Almond, 128, **129**
Cilantro Cream, 132, **133**
Cilantro Lime Vinaigrette, 198
Cilantro-Mint Purée, 178, **179**
Cilantro Sauce, Ginger-, 118, **119**

Cinnamon:
    Graham Cookie with Marshmallow
        Crème and Dark Chocolate
        Fondue, 94, **95**
    "Ice Cream," Spiced, 102, **103**
    Syrup, Coffee-, 186, **187**
    Vanilla Cream, 192, **193**
Citrus Cream, 190, **191**
Citrus Tart, 115
Cocoa Syrup, Black, 104, **105**
Coconut:
    Brittle, 47, **48**
    Crust, -Macaroon, 207
    Dumplings, White, 60, **61**
    "Rice," 166, **167**
    Sauce, 130, **131**
Coffee-Cinnamon Syrup, 186, **187**
Conch Chowder, Caribbean, **146,** 147
Confit, tomato, 50
Cookie/Cookies; see also Wafers
    Cinnamon Graham, with
        Marshmallow Crème, 94, **95**
    Fortune, 228, **229**
    Macaroons, Crispy Chile, 186, **187**
    Macaroons, Crispy Lime, 134, **135**
    Oreo, with Cream Filling, 104, **105**
Corn:
    Chowder, Yellow, 24, **25**
    Flan, Sweet, 186, **187**
    Tamale, White, 88, **89**
Cornbread Bruschetta, 182
Couscous, 120, **121**
Crackers, Black Sesame, 68, **69**
Cream, Banana Lemongrass, 72, **73**
Cream/Crème:
    Basil "Crème Fraîche," 162, **163**
    Cilantro, 132, **133**
    Cinnamon Vanilla, 192, **193**
    Citrus, 190, 191
    Eggplant and Hummus, 156, **157**
    Ginger, 46, 60, 70, **71**
    Marshmallow, 94, **95**
    Oregano, 97
    Sweet, 136, **137**
    Truffle, 82, **83**
    Vanilla Bean, 48, **49**
"Cream Cheese" Mini Tartlet, Blueberry
    and Sweet, 206
Cream Filling, Oreo Cookie with, 104,
    105. See also Susie Q

"Crème Fraîche," Basil, 162, **163**
Cream of Matsutake Soup, 26, **27**
Crêpes, Cacao, and Sweet Mint Custard
    with Black Cacao Sauce, 98, **99**
Crisps, Pignoli "Parmesan" 28
Crisps, Warm "Cheese," 80, **81**
Crumble, cashew, 42, **43**
Cuban Salad with Breaded Onion Rings
    and Cilantro Lime Vinaigrette, 198
Cucumber:
    Gazpacho, Golden Tomato and
        Lemon, 40, **41**
    Salad, Thai, 232, **233**
    Spiced, 114
Cumin Flatbread, 121–22, **121**
Curry:
    Froth, 126, **127**
    "Ice Cream," Red, 106
    Sauce, 130, **131**
    Sauce, Red Pepper, 68, **69**
Custard, Sweet Mint, 98, **99**

D

Dandelion Greens, Marinated, 172, **173**
Dashi Sake Broth, Sweet, Zaru Somen
    and, 212, **213**
Date Flan, Ginger, with Mint Syrup, 124,
    125
Dipping Sauce, Red Chili–Pineapple,
    196, **197**
Dolmas, Grape Leaf, Vegetables and,
    138, **139**
Dosas, White Raisin Shiitake, 132, **133**
Dressing, 155; see also Sauce;
    Vinaigrette
    Ginger, 223
    Lemon, Preserved, 116, **117**
    Miso-lime-almond, 196
    Tahini, Sweet, 56, **57**
Dumplings; see also Wrappers
    Pignoli, 26, **27**
    Red Pepper Almond Romesco, 172,
        173
    Sesame, Black, 60, **61**
    Sesame-Cashew, 200, **201**
    White Coconut, 60, **61**
Dust; see also Powder
    Lemon, 62, **63**
    of Three Leaves, 76, **77**
    Red bell pepper, 198

E

Eggplant and Hummus Cream in Almond Tart Shells, 156, **157**
Eggplant Bacon, 164, **165**
Elephant Roll, Inside-Out, with Chipotle Mayo, 204, 205
Empadinhas de Queijo, 202, **203**
Empanada de Espinaca y Tomate Relish, 178, **179**
Empanada with Spinach, 178, **179**
Empanadas, "Cheese," 202, **203**
Ensalada Criolla, Cebollas Fritas y Vinagreta Cubana, 198
Escabeche, Oyster-Mushroom, 74, **75**

F

Fava Bean Purée, 44, **45**
Fig Puree, Balsamic, 70, **71**
Flan:
    Corn, Sweet, 186, **187**
    Ginger Date, with Mint Syrup, 124, **125**
    Orange Pineapple, and Lime Syrup, 154
    Pumpkin, Frozen, 78, **79**
    Spinach-Striped Flan, 62, **63**
    Sweet Pea, 22, **23**
Flatbread. *See* Bread
Foam; *see also* Froth
    Cinnamon, 78, **79**
    Leek and Brazil Nut Truffle, 108, **109**
    Macadamia, 22, **23**
    White Cardamom, 62, **63**
"Foie Gras," Portobello, 65
Fondue:
    Dark Chocolate, 94, **95**
    Green Zebra, 32, 33
    Sweet Tamarind, 230, 231
Fortune Cookies, 228, **229**
Froth, Curry, 126, **127**
Fruits, Candied, with Longan Syrup, 214, **215**

G

Garlic and Onion Bread, 164, **165**
Garlic Flower "Yogurt," 158, **159**
Gazpacho, Golden Tomato and Lemon Cucumber, with Avocado Salsa, 40, **41**

"Gelato"; *see also* "Ice Cream"; Parfait
    Almond, 72, **73**
    Ginger Cantaloupe, and Watermelon Granité with Muscat Honeydew Puree, 34, **35**
Ginger:
    Cream, 46, **47,** 70, **71**
    Cream Sauce, 76, **77**
    Date Flan with Mint Syrup, 124, **125**
    Dressing, 223
    Marinara, Sun-Dried Tomato-, 160, **161**
    Pickled, 204, 205
    Raita, Banana-, 130, **131**
    Sauce, 224, **225**
    -Tomato Chutney, 132, **133**
Gnocchi, Arugula, 152, **153**
Gnocchi of Broccoli Rabe with Ginger Cream Sauce, 76, **77**
Goji Berry "Ice Cream," 218–20, **219**
Graham Cookie, Cinnamon, with Marshmallow Crème, 94, **95**
Granité, Watermelon, 34, **35**
Grape Chutney, Concord, 76, **77**
Grape Leaf Dolmas, Vegetables and, 138, **139**
Grapefruit-Infused Jicama "Rice," 64
Green Tea Canneloni, 72, **73**
Green Tea "Ice Cream," 218–20, **219**
Greens, Marinated, 82, **83**
Guacamole, 88, **89**

H

Hallacas Vegetarianas, 180, **181**
Harissa, **121,** 122
Hazelnut "Yogurt," 148, **149**
Herb Oil, Green, 44, **45**
Hijiki and Kohlrabi with Sweet Tahini Dressing, 56, **57**
Hijiki Caviar, 108, **109**
Honeydew, Muscat, Purée, 34, **35**
Hummus, 199
Hummus Cream, Eggplant and, in Almond Tart Shells, 156, **157**

I

"Ice Cream"; *see also* "Gelato"; Parfait
    Banana, 98
    Basil, 50, **51**

Canjica, 168–70, **169**
Goji Berry, 218–20, **219**
Green Tea, 218–20, **219**
Melting Olive Oil, 80, 81
Mochi, 218–20, **219**
Red Curry, 106
Rosewater, 115
Spiced Cinnamon, 102, **103**
Star Anise, 123
Vanilla Bean, 96, **97,** 104, **105**
Vanilla Lemongrass, 218–20, **219**

J

Jackson Pollock Raviolo with Arugula Pesto, 66, **67**
Jam, raspberry, 98
Jam, Sweet Tomato, 158, **159**
Jiaozi Three Ways, 221–23, **222**
Jicama:
    Broth, 164, **165**
    "Fried," 155
    "Rice," Grapefruit-Infused, 64

K

Kohlrabi, Hijiki and, with Sweet Tahini Dressing, 56, **57**
Kulfi, Cardamom, 134, **135**

L

Lavender Pie, Almond-, in Coconut-Macaroon Crust, 207
Leek and Brazil Nut Truffle Foam, 108, **109**
Lemon:
    Dressing, Preserved, 116, **117**
    Dust, 62, **63**
    Relish, Green Olive–Preserved, 172, **173**
Lemongrass Cream, Banana, 72, **73**
Lemongrass "Ice Cream," Vanilla, 218–20, **219**
Lime:
    -miso-almond dressing, 196
    Powder, 22, **23**
    Macaroon, Crispy, 134, **135**
    Sauce, Bitter Orange–, 194, **195**
    Sauce, Goji, 72, **73**
    Sauce, Sweet Chile–, 200, **201**
    Spiced Mango Chutney, 192, **193**
    Syrup, 154

Vinaigrette, Cilantro, 198
"Yogurt," Pickled, 128, **129**
"Longan" Syrup, 214, **215**
Lotus Root, Bok Choy with, 221–23, **222**

M

Macadamia:
    "Cheese," 30, **31**
    Foam, 22, **23**
    "Sour Cream," 184, **185**
Macaroon:
    Crispy Lime, 134, **135**
    Crust, Almond-Lavender Pie in
        Coconut-, 207
    Crispy Chile, 186, **187**
Manchego Paper, 76, **77**
Mango:
    Chutney, –Green Papaya, 114
    Chutney, Lime-Spiced, 192, **193**
    Pudding, Creamy, 134, **135**
    Salsa, Spicy, 216, **217**
    Terrine (almond-beet-mango), 64
Manti, Basil, 148, **149**
Marinara, Sun-Dried Tomato-Ginger,
    160, **161**
Marshmallow Whip, 100, **101**
Matsutake Soup, Cream of, 26, **27**
Mayo, Chipotle, 204, 205
"Meatballs," Portobello, 97
Mesquite, The Magic of, 170
Mesquite Truffles, 183
Mint:
    Chutney, -Almond, 128, **129**
    Custard, Sweet, 98, **99**
    Panna Cotta, Frozen, with
        Marshmallow Whip, 100, **101**
    Pesto, -Basil Pistachio, 160, **161**
    Purée, Cilantro-, 178, **179**
    Sauce, Cool 138–40, **139**
    Syrup, 124, **125**
Miso:
    Dressing (miso-lime-almond), 196
    Sauce, Creamy, 60, **61**
    Sauce, Tahini, 74, **75**
Mochi "Ice Cream," 218–20, **219**
Mole, Cacao, 188, **189**
Mole, Raw Cacao, 88, **89**
Moqueca, Shiitake, and Coconut "Rice,"
    166, **167**
Mousse, basil, 62

Mousse, spinach, 62
Muscat Honeydew Purée, 34, **35**
Mushrooms:
    Caramelized Shiitake with Bamboo
        Shoots, 221–23, **222**
    Chanterelle Essence, 28
    Cream of Matsutake Soup, 26, **27**
    Mushrooms and White Asparagus
        with Red Pepper Curry Sauce,
        68, **69**
    Oyster-Mushroom Escabeche, 74,
        75
    Oyster Mushroom Seviche, 194,
        195
    Oyster Mushrooms and Hijiki Caviar,
        108, **109**
    Portobello "Foie Gras," 65
    Portobello "Meatballs," 97
    Serrano-Spiced Portobello, 88, 89
    Sesame Enoki Mushrooms, 58, **59**
    Shiitake Moqueca and Coconut
        "Rice," 166, **167**
    Shiitake Ravioli, 70, **71**
    Trumpet Mushroom Salad, 58, **59**
    Sage-Pumpkin "Risotto," with
        Wild Mushrooms, 171
    White Raisin Shiitake Dosas, 132,
        133
Mustard sauce, 223

N

Natilla de Chocolate, Majarete y Turron
    de Coco, 186, **187**
Nigiri, Pickled Lotus, 204, 205
Nigiri, Sushi and, 204, 205
Noodles, Cold Spicy Long Life, with
    Ginger Sauce, 224, **225**
Noodles, Squash, 74, **75**

O

Ocean Vegetables and Squash Noodles
    with Oyster-Mushroom Escabeche,
    Faded Green Caviar, and Miso Tahini
    Sauce, 74, **75**
Oil, Basil, 38, **39**
Oil, Green Herb, 44, **45**
Olive Oil "Ice Cream," Melting, 80, **81**
Olive–Preserved Lemon Relish, Green,
    172, **173**
Olive Tapenade, Green, 156, **157**

Onion:
    Bread, Garlic and, 164, **165**
    Broth, Green, 58, **59**
    Rings, Breaded, 198
Orange Blossom Water Tart with Star
    Anise "Ice Cream," 123
Orange:
    Flan, Pineapple, and Lime Syrup, 154
    Powder, 90, **91**, 183
    Truffles, 183
    Sauce, Bitter, –Lime, 194, **195**
Oregano Cream, 97
Oreo Cookie with Cream Filling, 104,
    105
Oyster:
    -Mushroom Escabeche, 74, **75**
    Mushroom Seviche and Bitter
        Orange–Lime Sauce, 194, **195**
    Mushrooms and Hijiki Caviar, 108,
        109

P

Pancakes, Summer Summer, with Garlic
    Flower "Yogurt," 158, **159**
Panna Cotta, Frozen Mint, with
    Marshmallow Whip, 100, **101**
Papaya Chutney, Mango–Green, 114
Pappadam, Black Sesame, 126, **127**
Paratha, Black Sesame, 114
Parfait, Raspberry, 48, **49**. *See also*
    "Gelato"; "Ice Cream"
"Parmesan" Crisp, Pignoli, 28
"Parmesan," Pine Nut, 38, **39**, 152, **153**
Paste, Marcona Almond, 82, **83**
"Paul Smith" Basil, 62
Pavé, Heirloom Tomato, 116, **117**
Pea, Sweet, Flan, 22, **23**
Pea, Sweet, Samosas, 128, **129**
Pear Sauce, Wine, 150, **151**
Pearl Balls with Spicy Mango Salsa,
    216, **217**
Pears, 26, **27**
Pepper:
    Dumplings, Red, Almond Romesco,
        172, **173**
    Dust, red bell, 198
    Sauce, Aleppo, 138–40, **139**
    Sauce, Sweet, 152, **153**
    Soup, Roasted Sweet, 148, **149**
    Wrappers, Sweet, 82, **83**

Pesto, Arugula, 66, **67**
Pesto, Mint-Basil Pistachio, 160, **161**
Pho Broth, Vietnamese, with Tofu, 226, **227**
Picadillo Santiaguero, Arroz Amarillo, y Mariquitas, 184, **185**
Pie, Almond-Lavender, in Coconut-Macaroon Crust, 207
Pignoli:
    Dumplings, 26, **27**
    "Parmesan" Crisp, 28
    "Sour Cream," 92, **93**
Pine Nut:
    and Black Truffle "Ricotta," 160, **161**
    "Cheese," 90, **91**
    "Parmesan," 38, **39,** 152, **153**
    Tartlet, 162, **163**
Pineapple:
    Carpaccio, 155
    Dipping Sauce, Red Chili–, 196, **197**
    Flan, Orange, 154
Pinot Noir Sauce, 90, **91**
Pistachio:
    Pesto, Mint-Basil, 160, **161**
    Purée, 32, **33**
    Truffles, -Cacao, 183
    Tuiles, 136, **137**
Plaintain, Crisp, 184, **185**
Plum:
    Carpaccio, 46, **47**
    Cinnamon-Glazed, 36, **37**
    Syrup, Vanilla Bean–, 36, **37**
Portobello:
    "Foie Gras" on Sun-Dried Tomato Flatbread, 65
    "Meatballs," 97
    -Meat Stew, 184, **185**
    Serrano-Spiced, 88, **89**
Powder: *see also* Dust
    Lime, 22, **23.**
    Orange, 90, **91,** 183
Pudding:
    Chocolate, 186, **187**
    Chocolate, Frozen, 36, **37**
    Mango, Creamy, 134, **135**
Pudim de Leite, 168, **169**
Pumpkin Flan, Frozen, Cinnamon Foam, and Mandarin Candy, 78, **79**
Pumpkin "Risotto," Sage-, with Wild Mushrooms, 171

Purée:
    Balsamic Fig, 70, **71**
    Cilantro-Mint, 178, **179**
    Fava Bean, 44, **45**
    Mint-Basil Pistachio Pesto, 160, **161**
    Pistachio, 32, **33**
    Raviolini, 29
    Macadamia, 158
    Muscat Honeydew, 34, **35**

R

Rabe, Broccoli, 70, **71**
Rabe, Gnocchi of Broccoli, 76, **77**
Ragout of Spring Vegetables, 28
Raisin Shiitake Dosas, White, 132, **133**
Raita, Banana-Ginger, 130, **131**
Raspberry jam, 98
Raspberry:
    Parfait, 48, **49**
    Sauce, 106
    Sauce, Leaf–Infused Cherry, 115
    Sundae, 96, **97**
Ravioli:
    Beet, 44, **45**
    Bitter Broccoli, 90, **91**
    Shiitake, 70, **71**
    Spinach and Beet, 150, **151**
Raviolini, Basil, 29
Raviolini purée, 29
Raviolo with Arugula Pesto, Jackson Pollock, 66, **67**
Red Chili–Pineapple Dipping Sauce, 196, **197**
Red Pepper Curry Sauce, 68, **69**
Relish, Green Olive–Preserved Lemon, 172, **173**
Relish, Tomato, 178, **179**
"Rice":
    Ba Bao Fan Blessing Eight-Treasure 214, **215**
    Coconut, 166, **167**
    Grapefruit-Infused Jicama, 64
    with Coconut Sauce, 130, **131**
    Yellow, 184, **185**
"Ricotta," Cashew, 150, **151**
"Ricotta," Pine Nut and Black Truffle, 160, **161**
"Ricotta" Tart, Green Tomato–, 50, **51**
"Risotto," Sage-Pumpkin, with Wild Mushrooms, 171

Roll/Rolls:
    Inside-Out Elephant, with Chipotle Mayo, 204, 205
    Spicy "Fried" Spring, with Sweet Tamarind Fondue, 230, **231**
    Summer, and Red Chili–Pineapple Dipping Sauce, 196, **197**
    Romesco Dumplings, Red Pepper Almond, 172, **173**
Rosewater "Ice Cream," 115
Rothko Terriine and Grapefruit-Infused Jicama "Rice," 64

S

Saffron Avgolemono, 97
Saffron Broth, Creamy, 107
Sage-Pumpkin "Risotto," with Wild Mushrooms, 171
Sake Broth, Sweet Dashi, Zaru Somen and, 212, **213**
Salad:
    Cuban Salad, 198
    Marinated Tomato, 38, **39**
    Salpicao, 155
    Thai Cucumber, 232, **233**
    Trumpet Mushroom Salad, 58, **59**
Salsa; *see also* Dressing; Sauce
Avocado, 40, 41
Mango, Spicy 216, **217**
Samosas, Sweet Pea, 128, **129**
Sauce; *see also* Cream; Dressing; Syrup; Vinaigrette; Whip
    Aleppo Pepper, 138–40, **139**
    Bitter Orange–Lime, 194, **195**
    Bittersweet Cacao, 100, **101**
    Black Cacao, 98, **99**
    Caramel, 170
    Cashew, 221
    Chile, 230
    Chocolate, 168, **169**
    Coconut, 130, **131**
    Cool Mint, 138–40, **139**
    Creamy Miso, 60, **61**
    Curry, 130, **131**
    Dark Chocolate, 48, **49**
    Ginger, 224, **225**
    Ginger-Cilantro, 118, **119**
    Ginger Cream, 76, **77**
    Goji Lime, 72, **73**
    Miso Tahini, 74, **75**

Moqueca, 166, **167**
Mustard, 223
Pinot Noir, 90, **91**
Ragout, 28
Raspberry, 106
Raspberry Leaf–Infused Cherry,
     115
Red Chili–Pineapple Dipping Sauce,
     196, **197**
red pepper, 188
Red Pepper Curry, 68, **69**
Sweet Chile–Lime, 200, **201**
Sweet Pepper, 152, **153**
Tahini, 138–40, **139**
Tomato, 29
Tomato-Chile, 180, **181**
Umeboshi Wasabi, 204, **205**
Wine Pear, 150, **151**
Serrano-Spiced Portobello, 88, 89
Sesame:
     Brittle, 124, **125**
     Dumplings, Black, 60, **61**
     Dumplings, Cashew, and Sweet
          Chile-Lime Sauce, 200, **201**
     Crackers, Black, 68, **69**
     Pappadam, Black, 126, **127**
     Paratha, Black, 114
     Tuile, Black, 22, **23**
Seviche, Oyster Mushroom and Bitter
     Orange–Lime Sauce, Bitter, 194,
     195
Shiitake:
     Bisteeya with Ginger-Cilantro Sauce,
          118, **119**
     Caramelized, with Bamboo Shoots,
          221–23, **222**
     Dosas, White Raisin, 132, **133**
     Moqueca and Coconut "Rice," 166,
          167
     Ravioli with Broccoli Rabe, Balsamic
          Fig Puree, and Ginger Cream,
          70, **71**
Somen, Zaru, and Sweet Dashi Sake
     Broth, 212, **213**
Soup; see also Broth; Chowder
     Cream of Matsutake, 26, **27**
     Pepper, Roasted Sweet, 148, **149**
"Sour Cream":
     Cashew, 180
     Macadamia, 184, **185**

Pignoli, 92, **93**
     White Truffle, 182
Spinach:
     and Beet Ravioli, 150, **151**
     Empanada with, 178, **179**
     Marinated, in Tomato Tacos, 190
     Mousse, 62
     -Striped Flan, 62, **63**
     Wilted, 118, **119;**
     with Basil, 150, **151**
Spring Rolls, Spicy "Fried," with Sweet
     Tamarind Fondue, 230, **231**
Spring Vegetable:
     Tagine with Couscous, 120, **121**
     Ragout of, 28
     with Curry Sauce, 130, **131**
Squash Blossoms with Pistachio Purée,
     32, **33**
Squash:
     Noodles, 74, **75**
     Pancakes, Summer, with Garlic
          Flower "Yogurt," 158, **159**
     Pasta, Yellow, 107
Star Anise "Ice Cream," 123
Star Anise Syrup, 42, **43**
Summer Rolls and Red Chili–Pineapple
     Dipping Sauce, 196, **197**
Sundae, Raspberry, 96, **97**
Sushi and Nigiri, 204, 205
Sushi "rice," 204, 205
Susie Q (cake with cream filling), 106
Sweet-and-Sour Tofu with Spiced
     Cashews, 221–23, **222**
Sweet Pea Flan with Macadamia Foam,
     Lime Powder, and Black Sesame
     Tuile, 22, **23**
Sweet Pea Samosas, 128, **129**
Syrup; *see also* Cream; Sauce; Whip
     Anise, 136, **137**
     Black Cocoa, 104, **105**
     Black Cacao, 218–20, **219**
     Cayenne-Cacao, 102, **103**
     Chocolate Anise, 96, **97**
     Coffee-Cinnamon, 186, **187**
     Lime, 154
     "Longan", 214, **215**
     Mint, 124, **125**
     Star Anise, 42, **43**
     Vanilla-Agave, 46, **47**
     Vanilla Bean–Plum, 36, **37**

T
Tacos, Chocolate Chili, 92, **93**
Tacos, Tomato, 190, **191**
Tagine, Spring Vegetable, with Couscous,
     120, **121**
Tahini:
     Dressing, Sweet, 56, **57**
     Sauce, 138–40, **139**
     Sauce, Miso, 74, **75**
Tamale, White Corn, 88, **89**
Tamales, Vegetable, with Tomato-Chile
     Sauce, 180, **181**
Tamarind Fondue, Sweet, Spicy "Fried"
     Spring Rolls with, 230, **231**
Tamarind-Glazed Cherry Tomatoes, 126,
     127
Tapenade, Green Olive, 156, **157,** 199
Tarts/Tartlets:
     Blueberry and Sweet "Cream
          Cheese" Mini, 206
     Chocolate Ancho Chile, 192, **193**
     Citrus, 115
     Green Tomato–"Ricotta," 50, **51**
     Mediterranean Mini, 199
     Orange Blossom Water, with Star
          Anise "Ice Cream,"123
     Pine Nut, 162, **163**
     Shells, Almond, 156, **157**
Tartare, Avocado, 126, **127**
Tea Canneloni, Green, 72, **73**
Tea "Ice Cream," Green, 218–20, **219**
Terrine, beet, mango, and avocado, 64
Thai Cucumber Salad, 232, **233**
Tofu:
     Black-and-White, 58, **59**
     Sweet-and-Sour, with Spiced
          Cashews, 221–23, **222**
     Vietnamese Pho Broth with, 226,
          227
Tomates del Sol Taacos con Crema
     Citrico, 190, **191**
Tomato/Tomatoes:
     Sauce, Chile, 180, **181**
     Confit, 50
     Chutney, Ginger-, 132, **133**
     Gazpacho, and Lemon Cucumber,
          40, **41**
     Tart, "Ricotta," 50, 51
     Pavé, Heirloom, 116, **117**

Salad, Marinated, 38, **39**
Relish, 178, **179**
Spiced, 182
Sauce, Summer, 29
Flatbread, Sun-Dried, 65
Marinara, -Ginger, Sun-Dried, 160, **161**
Jam, Sweet, 158, **159**
Tacos, 190, **191**
Tamarind-Glazed Cherry, 126, **127**
Truffle/Truffles, 168, 183;
Cream, 82, **83**
Foam, Leek and Brazil Nut, 108, **109**
Orange, Pistachio-Cacao, and Mesquite, 183
"Ricotta," Pine Nut and Black, 160, **161**
"Sour Cream," White, 182
Tuile, Black Sesame, 22, **23**
Tuiles, Pistachio, 136, **137**

U

Umeboshi Wasabi Sauce, 204, **205**

V

Vanilla-Agave Syrup, 46, **47**
Vanilla:
Cream, Cinnamon, 192, **193**
Lemongrass "Ice Cream," 218–20, **219**
Wafers, 100, **101**
Vanilla Bean:
Cream, 48, **49**
"Ice Cream," 96, **97**, 104, **105**
–Plum Syrup, 36, **37**
Vegetable Tagine, Spring, with Couscous, 120, **121**
Vegetable Tamales with Tomato-Chile Sauce, 180, **181**
Vegetables and Grape Leaf Dolmas, 138, **139**
Vegetables, Ocean, and Squash Noodles, 75, **75**
Vegetables, Ragout of Spring, 28
Vegetables, Spring, with Curry Sauce, 130, **131**
Vietnamese Pho Broth with Tofu, 226, **227**
Vinaigrette, Cilantro Lime, 198. *See also* Dressing; Sauce

W

Wafers, Chocolate Basil, 36, **37**
Wafers, Vanilla, 100, **101**
Walnuts, Candied, 96, **97**
Wasabi Sauce, Umeboshi, 204, **205**
Watermelon Granité, 34, **35**
Whip, Marshmallow, 100, **101**
Wine Pear Sauce, 150, **151**
Wrappers, 26, 29, 30; *see also* Dumplings
Basil Black Pepper, 30, **31**
Basil Manti, 148, **149**
Cashew, 221, **222**
Chocolate, 90, **91**
Coconut, 70
Dumpling, 172

Raviolo, 66
Samosa, 128, 129
Spring Roll, 230
Sweet Pepper and Basil, 82, **83**

Y

Yellow "Rice," 184, **185**
"Yogurt" Cake, Apricot, 136, **137**
"Yogurt," Garlic Flower, 158, **159**
"Yogurt," Hazelnut, 148, **149**
"Yogurt," Pickled Lime, 128, **129**

Z

Zaru Somen and Sweet Dashi Sake Broth, 212, **213**

Metric Conversion Chart

Liquid and Dry Measures

U.S.	Canadian	Australian
¼ teaspoon	1 mL	1 ml
½ teaspoon	2 mL	2 ml
1 teaspoon	5 mL	5 ml
1 tablespoon	15 mL	20 ml
¼ cup	50 mL	60 ml
⅓ cup	75 mL	80 ml
½ cup	125 mL	125 ml
⅔ cup	150 mL	170 ml
¾ cup	175 mL	190 ml
1 cup	250 mL	250 ml
1 quart	1 liter	1 litre

Temperature Conversion Chart

Fahrenheit	Celsius
250	120
275	140
300	150
325	160
350	180
375	190
400	200
425	220
450	230
475	240
500	260